101

Pistol Option Plays

James Vint

COACHES
CHOICE™

ISBN: 978-1-60679-227-8
Library of Congress Control Number: 2012939707
Cover design: Studio J Art & Design
Book layout: Studio J Art & Design
Front cover photo: ©Dennis Wierzbicki/Cal Sport Media/ZUMA Press

Coaches Choice
P.O. Box 1828
Monterey, CA 93942
www.coacheschoice.com

Dedication

This book is dedicated to the great men who have impacted me throughout my life: James Vint Sr., Thomas F. Vint, Jack Combs, Dr. Charles Daniel, Cicero Daniel, David Diaz, and Jerry Campbell.

Acknowledgments

I have been blessed to have been around tremendous coaches and mentors, without whom this book would not be possible. First and foremost, I want to thank my Lord and Savior, Jesus Christ, for making the ultimate sacrifice so we could have eternal salvation. Without Him, nothing would be possible.

My mother and father, Sandra and James Sr., provided me with a tremendous upbringing, and I cannot ever thank them enough. My wife, Mary Blake, was wonderful as she supported me through this entire process that required long nights and sore fingers. Jim Peterson helped guide me through the process and helped set this all into motion. Kristi Huelsing and Angie Perry were patient and supportive from start to finish. My coaching mentors, David Diaz and Jerry Campbell, encouraged me throughout the writing of this book.

I have been blessed to work with great coaches who are an inspiration to those around them. Kent Jackson, Mike Meeks, Blake Sandford, and Mark Ball bring out the best in kids and other coaches. My high school football coach, Craig Parkinson, has been a mentor to me throughout my coaching career. Each and every coach I have worked with has helped me to become a better role model and leader of our young people.

Contents

Preface

I have had the opportunity to coach football during three different decades. Our profession is unique in that so many are willing to share their knowledge and experience. Because of the hard work of so many coaches, I have had the good fortune of being able to learn some concepts that we have had some success with at both the high school and college levels. It is a pleasure to be able to share these concepts with others.

My hope with this book is that each of you can take some of what is written on the following pages and apply it to your program. This volume is by no means an exhaustive book of option plays that can be run from the pistol. It is, however, a collection of 101 of our most successful pistol option plays. If this book helps you put more points on the scoreboard, it will be considered a success.

1

Formations and Motions

The pistol offense gives you an opportunity to run multiple formations with diverse personnel groups. By using multiple formations, the offense can keep the defense off-balance. Your ultimate goal is to gain leverage on the defense at the point of attack. By using a variety of formations, you can force the defense to have to make adjustments, rather than simply lining up in their base front.

One of the biggest dilemmas facing coaches is how to keep the verbiage simple. Play calls can get very wordy. Because of this, the formations will be kept short using a word and a number. The word identifies the strength and type of formation. The number tells the fullback where he will align. Your fullback will be your adjuster in the pistol offense.

If the word in the formation begins with an R, the strength of the formation will be to the right. If the word in the formation begins with L, the strength will go to the left. The number in the formation call tells the fullback where he will align. The numbers correspond somewhat with traditional hole numbering. The following shows the different alignments for the fullback based on the number called. Because the tight end is to the right, the formation would be named with an R word.

In the pistol, the offensive line will use two-foot splits. However, you can adjust these splits as needed based on the concepts you are running. The quarterback will align at 4.5 yards from the center. Doing so gives the quarterback depth in the pass game, while allowing him to execute the entire run game effectively. The tailback will align directly behind the quarterback at eight yards. His depth can be adjusted as needed. When you install any offensive system, it is important to remember these are just guidelines. There are teaching alignments, and then there are ability alignments. Ability alignments are adjustments you will make based on the ability of your players. Be flexible so you can take advantage of the strengths of your personnel.

The base formation set with a tight end in the game is Rip/Liz. Rip puts the tight end to the right with his hand down. Liz puts the tight end to the left. By adding a number based on the example in Figure 1-1, the fullback will be told where to line up. Rip 2 puts the tight end to the right and the fullback lined up behind the right tackle. Rip 4 would put the fullback aligned one yard outside the tight end and one yard off the line of scrimmage. Liz would move the tight end to the left side of the formation. In Figure 1-2, the call is Rip 2. Rip puts the tight end to the right with his hand down. The number 2 tells the fullback to align at the depth of the quarterback, directly behind the right offensive tackle.

In addition to Rip and Liz, other words can be used to change the position of the Y. Ron and Lou align the Y as a twin receiver, off the line of scrimmage. Ray and Lee tell the Y to line up as a tight end, and the X and Z both to align opposite the tight end. This is the typical twins closed look. R and L align the Y as a slot. Finally, Rex and Lex tell the offense you are aligning in a bunch set. Figure 1-3 shows Lou 6, which is a typical 2x2 formation call for the offense.

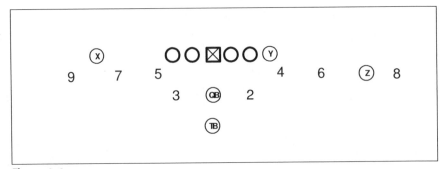

Figure 1-1

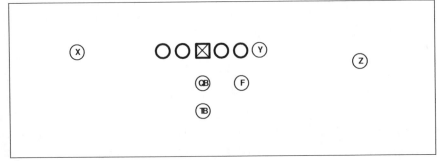

Figure 1-2

If the offense wanted to line up in a trips formation, they would put the fullback and the Y to the same side. Using Rip/Liz or Ron/Lou, the offense can align in a trips formation to either side. Rip 6 puts the fullback as a twin receiver to the side of the tight end, as displayed in Figure 1-4.

As you can see, aligning in a variety of formations is very simple. This system allows the offense to communicate hundreds of formation concepts with very simple verbiage. You can align in any formation imaginable using this system of R and L words combined with numbers. You can also tag special formations. Wing tells the Z to align one yard outside the tight end, one yard off the line of scrimmage. Figure 1-5 shows Liz 3 wing.

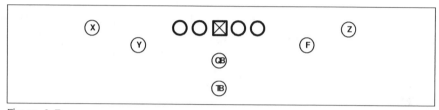

Figure 1-3

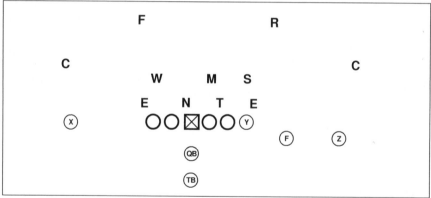

Figure 1-4

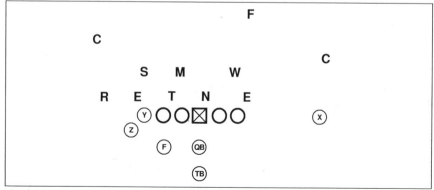

Figure 1-5

Once you have set your formations, you will need to have a simple way to use motion. You need to incorporate motion into your offense for several reasons:

- Force the defense to declare their coverage.
- Gain leverage on a defender.
- Force the defense to flip personnel.
- Make the defense change their strength.
- Create a mismatch.
- Flood one side of the field.
- Remove a defender from the point of attack.
- Bring an additional blocker to the point of attack.

Communicating motion can be very simple for you and your coaches. The system you will see depicted is very simple for communicating motion with players. This system is phonetic, which often is much easier for players to remember. Despite being simple, it has a built-in way to communicate movement for nearly every skill player.

Y Motions

- *Trade*: Flips the Y from one side to the other
- *Yip:* Y into the formation
- *Yap:* Y across the formation
- *Yop:* Y to the outside

Fullback Motions

- *Fip:* Fullback into the formation
- *Fap:* Fullback across the formation
- *Fop:* Fullback to the outside
- *Fox:* Fullback outside the X
- *Foz:* Fullback outside the Z

Z Motions

- *Zip:* Z into the formation
- *Zap:* Z across the formation
- *Zop:* Z to the outside

T Motions

- *Tip:* Tailback into the formation
- *Tap:* Tailback across the formation
- *Top:* Tailback to the outside
- *Tox:* Tailback outside the X
- *Toz:* Tailback outside the Z

As you can see, the motion terminology is very consistent from one position to the next. This makes it very easy for skill players to be able to play multiple positions. Ultimately, you want to keep things simple, allowing your athletes to play fast. In Figure 1-6, you will see zap motion, which tells the Z to go across the formation. The call in the huddle would be Rip 2 zap.

With this simple phonetic system, you can put any of your skill players in motion from anywhere on the field. This system allows your players to align in multiple positions and not have to learn a new motion call for each position. If you want to motion the fullback to the outside, you would tag the motion as fop, which is depicted in Figure 1-7.

Making your formation and motion rules simple allows you to be able to be multiple on offense. This allows you to gain leverage on the defense at the point of attack. You can use virtually any word you want to communicate with your players about where to line up. By keeping your formation and motion system simple, you will be more multiple on offense. You force defenses to have more to prepare for each week. The more a defense has to prepare for, the less time they have to spend on each aspect of your offense.

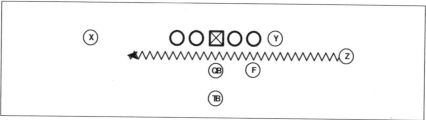

Figure 1-6

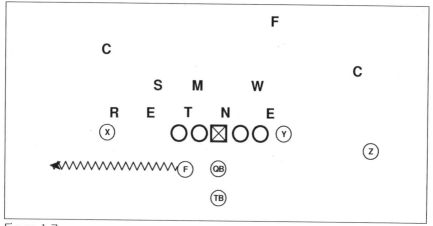

Figure 1-7

2

Midline Concepts

The midline is an option play that attacks the midpoint of the defense. The midline concept can be run several different ways from the pistol, and puts pressure on the defense's A and B gap defenders. The midline is a quick hitting play, and due to the closeness of the read to the quarterback, is perhaps the easiest option play to install.

When running the midline, the offense will not block the first player outside the playside guard. Versus an over front, this player will typically be the 3 technique. Initially, the midline was only run versus the over front, and was run to force the defense to reduce the 3 technique to a 1 technique, opening up the perimeter. The midline can also be run against odd fronts as well.

The midline option has very simple rules for the offensive line. When initially building the play, the offensive line learns they are responsible for their gap away from the playside. This responsibility adjusts slightly based on the different variations of the midline. Versus an even front, the midline will initially be run to a 3 technique or wider. The playside guard will inside release to block the A gap backer. The center will be responsible for the backside A gap player, who will usually be a 1 technique or 2i. The backside guard has the backside B gap player. The backside tackle has the backside C gap player. To create movement, anytime the defense gives the offense a 1 and 5 technique to the backside, the offense can have the center and backside guard combo the 1 technique to the backside backer. If the backside backer walks up to blitz the B gap, the guard would stay base on him, and the center would stay base on the 1 technique.

On the playside, the guard releases to the backer. The tackle and tight end will adjust their blocking assignments based on the call. The base midline scheme is run versus a 3 and 9 technique to the playside. The tackle will release up to the backer, and the tight end will base block the 9 technique. If the defense has a 7 technique, the offense will make a fold call. This will put the tackle blocking out on the 7 technique, and the tight end folding and tracking the playside linebacker. One important coaching point for the playside guard is to reduce his shoulder to get underneath the 3 technique. If he doesn't reduce his shoulder, he will get washed down and will not get vertical. One way to teach this is called "picking grass." He must reduce his shoulder and pick up grass. This is a technique taught by option guru Jerry Campbell, and it works very well for teaching this skill.

Two Tracking Two

The two-tracking-two concept is perhaps the most important concept to understand in the installation of the option attack. The offense always wants to have two players tracking the playside linebacker. In the base scheme, the playside guard and tackle will track the playside linebacker to the free safety. If the linebacker comes to you, you block him. If he goes away, you climb to the safety. In the fold scheme, the tight end and playside guard will track the playside linebacker to the safety. Figure 2-1 illustrates the two-tracking-two concept with the Mike backer attacking the dive. This puts the playside guard on the Mike backer, and the tackle working up to the free safety.

It is important that both players tracking the playside linebacker have their eyes on him. In Figure 2-2, the playside linebacker works to the B gap. Since the playside guard sees the linebacker go away, he climbs to the free safety. The playside tackle has the playside linebacker coming to him, so he blocks the playside linebacker.

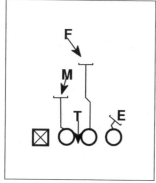

Figure 2-1

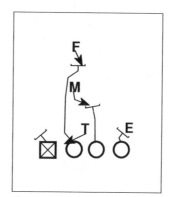

Figure 2-2

Figure 2-3 shows the two-tracking-two concept from the fold scheme. The tight end is now the second player tracking the playside linebacker to the safety. In Figure 2-3, the Mike linebacker steps to the playside guard. The playside guard will block the Mike, and the tight end will climb to the safety.

Figure 2-4 shows the fold scheme with the Mike linebacker working to the tight end. The playside guard sees the Mike backer going away from him, so he will climb to the free safety. The tight end will block the Mike linebacker.

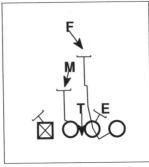

Figure 2-3   Figure 2-4

Backfield Action

The aiming point for the fullback is to run directly through the midpoint of the center. The fullback will make a deep, soft pocket with his arm closest to the quarterback up. A very good coaching point is to coach the running back to have his palm out because it keeps the elbow up. Another key is that the fullback must stay on the midpoint until something blocks his path. If the play is blocked correctly, no defender will get in his path. If the fullback comes off the midpoint too soon, the execution of the play is much more difficult.

There are several ways to utilize the quarterback's footwork. The three keys for your quarterback are to get off the midpoint, reach the ball deep, and get his eyes to his read. The easiest way to do this is to teach the quarterback to push away and step to get his feet parallel. He pushes away with his foot opposite the call, then steps to get his feet parallel with his playside foot. His first step should be a six-inch step, and his second step should bring his feet to a balanced position with the feet under the hips. The quarterback will then reach the ball deep to mesh with the back on his back leg. He gets his eyes to his read while he rides the back. He will make his decision at his front leg. If he is unsure at his front leg, teach him to give the football. The offset back can either be the pitchman, or the lead for the quarterback. The offset back can also be the dive back, but it is vital he stay on the midpoint.

The quarterback's read on the midline is very simple. He will read the intention of the read player. If the read player squeezes the dive, the quarterback will put the football and replace the read. The terminology to use to teach this skill is: "squeeze and chase, pull and replace." If the read player does anything else, give the football. The read must be drilled over and over for the quarterback to become effective with the read. Figure 2-5 shows the mesh between the quarterback and running back. The defensive tackle comes upfield, so the quarterback gives the football to the running back.

Figure 2-6 illustrates the defensive tackle squeezing and chasing the dive back. The quarterback's rule is squeeze and chase, pull and replace, so he will pull the football and replace the read player. This means the quarterback will run downhill through the vacated B gap.

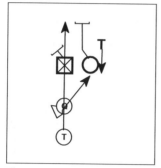 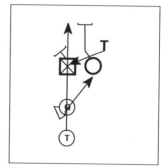

Figure 2-5   Figure 2-6

Mesh Drill

Perhaps the most important drill the offense can work to become good at running any option play is the mesh drill. The mesh drill is a five-minute drill with quarterbacks and running backs. The quarterbacks who are not in the drill will be the snapper or the read player. This drill gives the quarterbacks and running backs an opportunity to get better at the mesh, while helping the quarterbacks to improve their ability to make good reads.

Active Mesh Drill

The active mesh drill is a five-minute half-line period with the quarterbacks, running backs, and offensive line. The offensive players who are not in the drill act as the scout players on defense. The active mesh drill gives you a chance to work at various speeds with your players, helping them to become adept at running each of your option plays.

MIDLINE OPTION PLAYS

Play #1: Rip 2 Midline Option Right (Base)

Description: This play is the midline to the right side. Because the defense is playing with a 3 and 9 technique, the offense will use the base scheme. The playside guard and playside tackle will track the Mike backer up to the free safety. The offset back will block the Sam linebacker in the case of a quarterback pull.

Coaching Points:

- The playside guard must reduce his shoulder to get a free release to the backer.
- The center and backside guard must get movement on the 1 technique.
- The tailback must stay on path.

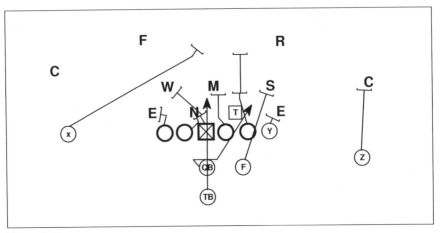

Figure 2-7

Play #2: Rip 7 Midline Right (Fold)

Description: Rip 7 puts the fullback aligned as a twin receiver opposite the tight end. You can use your fullback, or you can bring a receiver into the game. With the fullback aligned opposite the tight end, the defense must either rotate their secondary or adjust the front. Figure 2-8 shows the fold scheme being run on the frontside as the defense has rotated their secondary weak. The read is the exact same for the quarterback.

Coaching Points:

- The tailback must stay on the midpoint.
- The quarterback will read the 3 technique.
- The center and backside guard will combo the backside 1 technique to the Will backer.

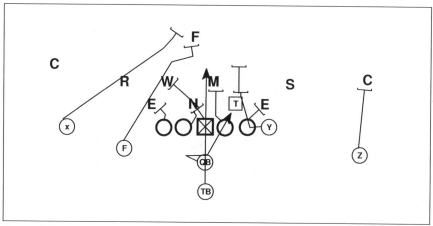

Figure 2-8

Play #3: Liz 3 Bone Midline Right (Weak)

Description: The midline is a great play to run from three-back sets as well. Typically, the midline would be checked to the side of the 3 technique. Being a three-back set means the offset back weak can become the second player tracking the playside backer if the play is run away from the tight end, as depicted in Figure 2-9. The backside back comes around to be the pitchman. He will call, "Ball, ball" as he runs his pitch path. Because of the tight path of the quarterback into the B gap, the ball will rarely be pitched.

Coaching Points:

- The formation call puts the fullback to the left and the halfback offset right.
- The reads for the quarterback remain the same.
- The halfback and the playside guard track the playside backer to the free safety.

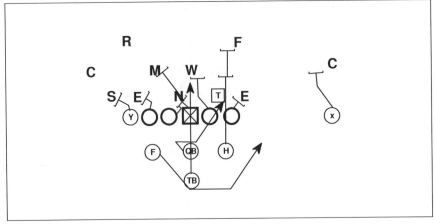

Figure 2-9

Play #4: Liz 3 Bone Midline Left (Base)

Description: If the defense puts the 3 technique to the strongside, the quarterback will check the play to that side. Because the tight end is the second player tracking the playside inside backer to safety, the offset back will be responsible for isolating the Sam backer. Figure 2-10 illustrates the midline to the tight end side from the bone.

Coaching Points:

- The quarterback will read the 3 technique.
- The quarterback will use the "squeeze and chase, pull and replace" rule.
- With a 3 and 9 technique strongside, the offense will work the base scheme.

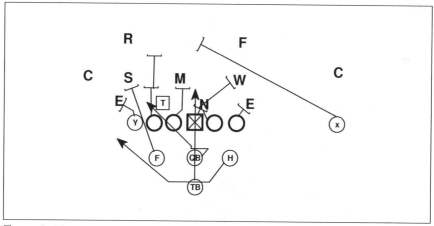

Figure 2-10

Play #5: R 2 Tom Midline Left

Description: With the tight end aligned in a slot position, he can be motioned to the playside, which is called tom. This means whichever way the quarterback checks the play, the tom will motion that way. The quarterback will always run the midline away from the reduction, and in Figure 2-11 he would check the play to the left. He then would tap his foot to put the tight end in motion. The tight end would then motion to the center, and then shuffle his feet and square his body as he motions to the B gap. The tight end and tackle work this just like the fold scheme. This motion allows the offense to get another blocker at the point of attack.

Coaching Points:

- The Y will shuffle once he crosses the center.
- The quarterback will call for the snap as the Y gets behind the playside guard.
- The fullback will become the pitchman for the quarterback.

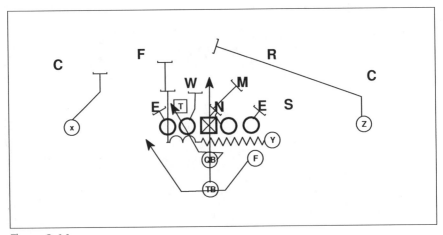

Figure 2-11

Play #6: R 2 Fom Midline Left

Description: The same concept can be worked with the fullback motioning to the playside. This is called "fom" motion. The fullback will use the same motion techniques as the Y used in tom motion. The fullback then becomes the second player, tracking the playside linebacker to the safety.

Coaching Points:

- The offensive line will block midline the same way.
- The quarterback reads remain unchanged.
- With no pitch key, the play becomes a double option.

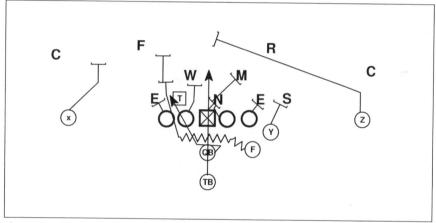

Figure 2-12

Play #7: Rip 2 Midline Right vs. Odd Front

Description: The midline can also be run versus odd front defenses. With a head-up nose, the quarterback will check the play to the widest defensive tackle. Typically, the read will be a 4 or 5 technique. Because of the distance of the read, it may appear the quarterback will always give the ball. The read, however, often will run the heel line to play the back. The quarterback must get his eyes to his read and not change his mechanics. Versus an odd front, the offense will typically use the base scheme. The playside tackle will release to the playside backer. The center and both guards will combo the noseguard to the backside backer. If the backside backer attacks the backside B gap, the backside guard will come off and block him. If the backside linebacker flows over the top, the playside guard will come off the combo to block him. The center will stay on the nose. The dive back will run up the heels of the center and make one cut based on the block on the noseguard. Figure 2-13 depicts the midline versus an odd front.

Coaching Points:

- The tailback must have his eyes on the block on the nose.
- The quarterback will read the first player past the playside guard, which is the 5 technique, in this case.
- The backside guard will adjust his block based on the alignment of the backside down defenders.

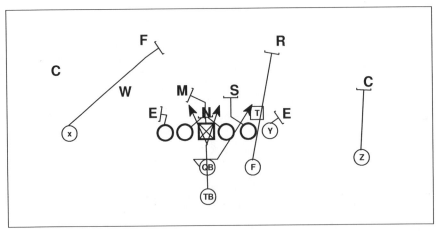

Figure 2-13

Play #8: Rip 3 Midline Left (Weak)

Description: With the fullback offset to the weakside, the offense has a second player to track the playside linebacker to the free safety if the play is run weak. The defense often will reduce their front to the tight end, which puts the 3 technique to the weakside. This means the offense can run the play to the split side. Figure 2-14 illustrates the midline weak.

Coaching Points:

- Your fullback will get his eyes to the playside linebacker.
- The quarterback will read the 3 technique for his give/keep read.
- The mechanics of the play do not change.

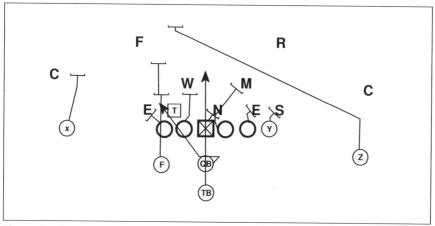

Figure 2-14

Play #9: R 5 Midline Right

Description: The midline can also be run from the pistol with a double slot set. The tight end can be replaced with another running back, just like in the bone formation. The quarterback reads do not change. The play can be checked either way based on the alignment of the defense. The frontside slot will be the fold player up to the playside inside backer. The backside back will be the pitchman. Because of the depth of the quarterback, the pitchman does not have to go in motion. He must be quick, but he has time to get into pitch relationship.

Coaching Points:

- The backside slot will be the pitchman.
- The frontside slot will be the fold player.
- The mechanics of the play do not change.

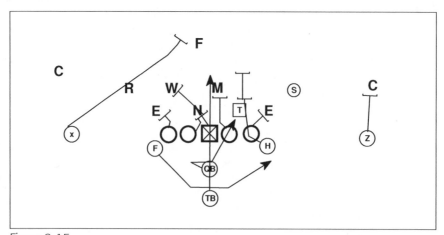

Figure 2-15

MIDLINE COMPLEMENTS

The defense must make adjustments to defend the midline. If your offense is blocking the play well, and the quarterback is making good reads, the defense will rely on players folding fast to make the play. This requires the offense have some answers to take advantage of defenders vacating their gap responsibilities. Additionally, these complements allow the offense to dictate who carries the football.

Play #10: Rip 3 Midline Pitch Right

Description: The pitch scheme takes advantage of an outside linebacker falling into the midline play, vacating his force responsibility. Pitch tells the offensive line they will not block the read player, or the next adjacent down defender outside the read player. The tight end will arc release to the outside linebacker if the play is being run strong. Figure 2-16 illustrates the pitch scheme.

Coaching Points:

- Your tight end must rip-and-reach and get his eyes on the force player.
- The quarterback will widen his path slightly on a pull read.
- The fullback must get into pitch relationship quickly.

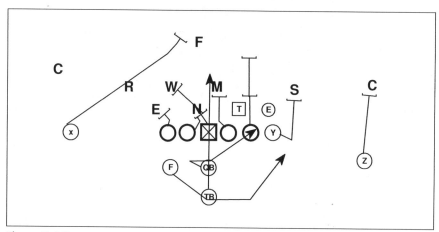

Figure 2-16

Play #11: Rip 2 Midline Pitch vs. an Odd Front

Description: The pitch scheme can also be run versus an odd front defense as well. The tackle will release to the playside inside backer, while the center and frontside guard will combo to the backside inside backer. Depending on the technique of the backside defensive end, the backside guard could work with the center and right guard. The tight end will arc up to the rotated invert. Figure 2-17 shows the pitch scheme versus an odd front.

Coaching Points:

- The quarterback will read the 5 technique for his dive read.
- The end defender on the line will be the pitch key.
- The fullback must be quick to get into pitch relationship.

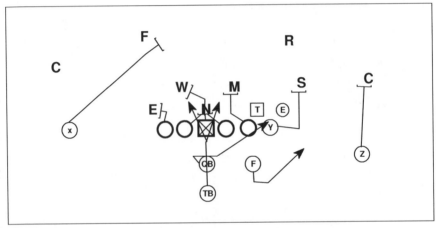

Figure 2-17

Play #12: Rip Midline Pitch Left (Weak)

Description: The pitch scheme can be run to the weak side as well. The guard will inside release to the playside backer, while the playside tackle will outside release and work up to the first player in an opposite-colored jersey. The fullback will become the pitchman, and can be aligned playside or opposite. If he is playside, he will drop-step and get into pitch relationship. He must be patient to allow the quarterback time to ride the fullback and read the 3 technique. The pitch scheme takes advantage of force players who quickly fall into the box on a pull read by the quarterback. Figure 2-18 illustrates the pitch scheme weak.

Coaching Points:

- The fullback must be patient so he doesn't get in front of the quarterback.
- The quarterback read stays the same.
- The receivers must do a great job of blocking the perimeter.

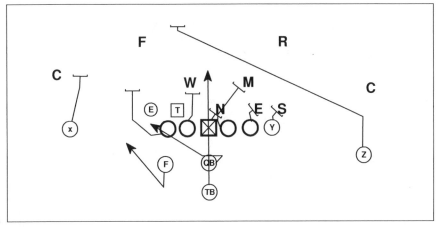

Figure 2-18

Play #13: R 5 Midline Pitch Right (Crack)

Description: The pitch scheme can also be run with a crack tag. The crack tag puts the halfback working to the corner, and the playside receiver cracking the invert. This is a great scheme to create a running lane when you anticipate the ball will be pitched. Figure 2-19 illustrates the pitch crack scheme.

Coaching Points:

- The Z-receiver will crack the inverted player or near safety.
- The quarterback read will not change.
- The backside fullback will become the pitchman.

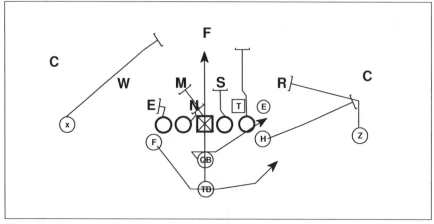

Figure 2-19

Play #14: R 2 Fullback Midline Pitch Right

Description: The offset back can also be the dive back, which is denoted by adding "fullback" to the play call. The tailback will become the pitchback. The blocking does not change. The slot to the playside will arc release up to the invert.

Coaching Points:

- The fullback will step to the quarterback to mesh and attack the near leg of the center.
- The tailback will become the pitchman.
- The offensive line will block the pitch scheme the same way regardless of who the dive back will be.

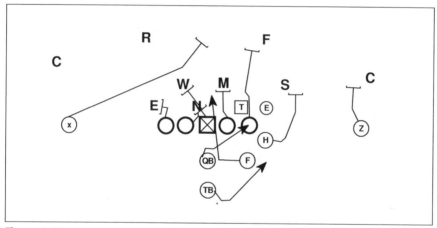

Figure 2-20

Play #15: Rip 3 Follow Opposite

Description: When the Will linebacker begins to work quickly over the combination block and tackles the fullback at three yards, the follow opposite play is a good call. On the follow opposite play, the quarterback will ride the dive back through the mesh. When the mesh disengages, the dive back bends backside and blocks the first opposite-colored jersey. If the backside linebacker vacates, the back will block the next defender who shows. The quarterback will pull the football and follow the dive back. The playside guard will block the read key, as the quarterback will not be reading a defender. Figure 2-21 illustrates the follow opposite play.

Coaching Points:

- The tailback will block backside after the mesh.
- The fullback still runs his pitch path.
- The quarterback must sell the midline action before bending backside.

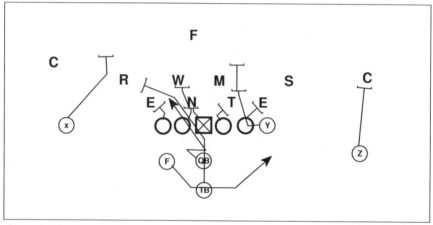

Figure 2-21

Play #16: Rip 2 Follow Opposite

Description: The follow opposite play can be run in a variety of ways. The frontside can sell the pitch action or pitch crack action as well. Figure 2-22 shows the follow opposite scheme with crack action from the tight end and corner.

Coaching Points:

- The guard must block the dive read key to secure the backside.
- The fullback still runs his pitch path.
- The quarterback must sell the midline action before bending backside.

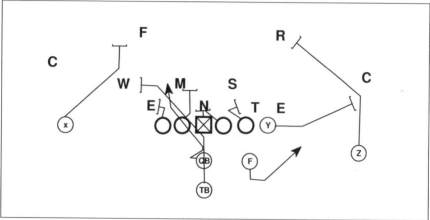

Figure 2-22

Play #17: Rip 2 Tailback Trap Right

Description: To stop the option game, some defenses will have the 3 technique hunker down at the line of scrimmage. They will not commit to the dive back or the quarterback. If the 3 technique hunkers down at the line of scrimmage, the offense can run trap off midline action, which is a called give. The backside guard will trap the player who would normally be read.

Coaching Points:

- The offense will trap block the play.
- The quarterback will give the football after a long ride.
- The quarterback will check the backside backer to see how he reacts to the play.

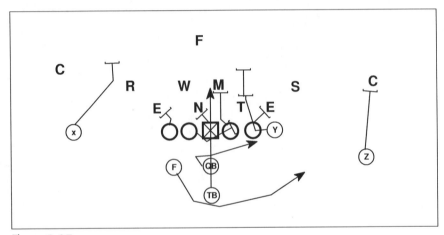

Figure 2-23

Play #18: Rip 2 Trap Read Opposite

Description: Another variation is the trap read opposite. The backside guard will trap the player who would normally be read. The quarterback will read the backside inside linebacker. If the backside inside linebacker crosses the midpoint of the defense, the quarterback will pull the ball and run through the vacated B gap. If the Will stays home, the quarterback will give the football. Figure 2-24 shows this concept versus an odd front defense.

Coaching Points:

- The offense will trap block the play.
- The tight end and tackle will block fold or base, depending on the technique of the defender.
- The quarterback must get his eyes to the Will backer.

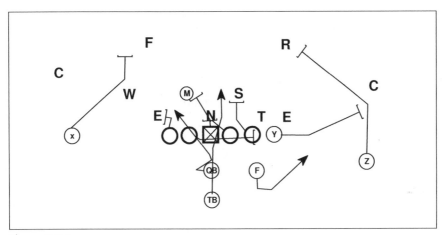

Figure 2-24

Play #19: Rip 3 Trap Read Opposite Fullback Lead

Description: The offense can also have the fullback align to the backside, and rather than be a pitchman, the fullback can replace the pulling guard and lead up on the backside inside backer. If the backside inside backer mirrors the trap, the fullback will work to the next opposite-colored jersey. Figure 2-25 illustrates the trap read opposite with the fullback leading backside.

Coaching Points:

- The offense will trap block the play.
- The fullback will lead up on the first opposite-colored jersey.
- The quarterback must make the play look exactly like midline.

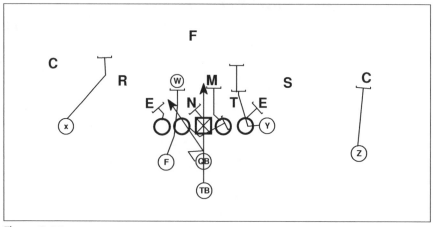

Figure 2-25

3

Veer Concepts

The veer is an option play that allows the defense to quickly attack the B, C, and D gaps. Run as a triple option, the veer has three possible ballcarriers each play. The inside and outside veer plays provide the offense with opportunities to get the ball into the hands of good athletes in open space.

The inside veer is a quick hitting option play that attacks the B gap of the defense. Like the midline, the quarterback will have a player he will be reading. The offensive line rules are very simple for the inside veer. They will block gap away. While the offense has the ability to man block gap away, zone combination blocks can be much more effective. Linemen will work in tandem blocking a down defender and tracking a linebacker.

With the inside veer play, the offense will be reading the first player on or outside the playside tackle. This will usually be a 5 technique. The running back will aim for inside hip of the guard while working downhill. The quarterback will step at 45 degrees with his playside foot, and bring his second step to a near parallel position. He will reach the ball deep to mesh with the back, and ride the back into the hole. The rule for the quarterback is the same as the midline as to whether he will give the football to the back: "Squeeze and chase, pull and replace." If the player he is reading squeezes and plays the back, pull the football, get downhill, and replace the read defender. If he does anything else, give the football.

Veer Blocks

The veer blocking at the point of attack is crucial to the success of the play. The tackle is always going to block the B gap away from the call. If the B gap has a down defender, the tackle will make a tandem call with the guard. This call puts the tackle and the guard working together to knock the down defender into the linebacker. If there is no down defender in the B gap, the tackle will inside release to the inside backer. Like the midline, the tackle in veer needs to reduce his shoulder so he doesn't get slammed down by the defensive end. Figure 3-1 illustrates a combination block between the guard and the tackle as the B gap is covered. Figure 3-2 shows the inside release of the tackle to the linebacker, as the B gap is not filled with a down defender.

Another release for the playside tackle is the outside veer or arc release. The tackle will drop-step with his outside foot to gain depth. Then he will crossover and rip through to gain enormous width. Figure 3-3 illustrates an outside release by the tackle.

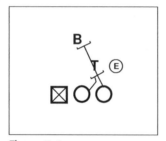

Figure 3-1

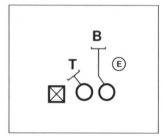

Figure 3-2

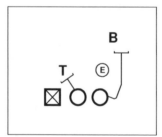

Figure 3-3

Two Tracking Two

The two-tracking-two concept used with the midline option carries over to the veer option as well. The offense can have a second player tracking the playside linebacker to free safety. This can be the Y, the fullback, or a receiver. The offense has the versatility to show the defense several different looks, while finding new ways to gain leverage on the defense.

In Figure 3-4, the playside tackle and the second player tracking the playside linebacker to safety both have their eyes on the playside backer. The playside backer steps up into the B gap, meaning the playside tackle will block him. The second player tracking the playside backer then climbs to the free safety.

Figure 3-5 shows the playside backer working outside in a gap exchange. The playside tackle sees him going away and climbs to linebacker. The playside slot player will now block the playside linebacker.

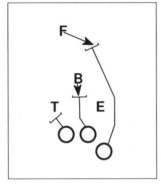

Figure 3-4

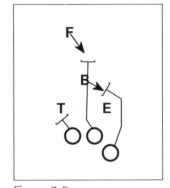

Figure 3-5

Play #20: Liz 2 Inside Veer Right

Description: The veer play is first installed to the openside of the defense. The offense will read the C gap defender, typically a 5 technique. In the two-back pistol, the fullback and the tailback can be the dive back. Figure 3-6 shows the inside veer play from a two-back pistol look versus an overshift 4-3 defense. The playside tackle will take the best release to the playside backer. If the defensive end is wide, the playside tackle will use an inside release. If the defensive end is tight, the playside tackle will use an outside release. With the fullback being the dive back, the tailback will be the pitch player.

Coaching Points:

- The offensive line will use zone combination blocks.
- The quarterback will step at 45 degrees and get up into the hole.
- The quarterback must get his eyes to his read and reach the ball deep.

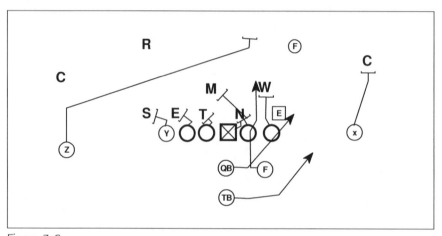

Figure 3-6

Play #21: Liz 2 Inside Veer Right vs. Under Front

Description: When the offense runs inside veer versus an under front, the B gap is covered by the 3 technique. The playside tackle and guard will double-team the 3 technique to the playside backer. The center and backside guard will combo the backside tackle to the backside backer. The fullback will read the 3 technique for his cut. The quarterback will read the 5 technique to determine whether to give or pull the football.

Coaching Points:

- The back must press the heels of the combo on the 3 technique.
- The quarterback must get his eyes to his read.
- The tailback must get into pitch relationship.

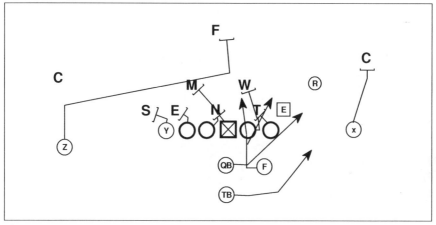

Figure 3-7

Play #22: Liz 3 Inside Veer Right vs. Bear

Description: The inside veer is a great play versus the Bear or double Eagle defense. Because the double Eagle and 46 Bear defenses tend to overshift to the strongside, the inside veer can give the offense leverage to the openside. The key block is the center's block on the noseguard. He must keep the noseguard from penetrating the playside A gap. Figure 3-8 shows the inside veer versus the double Eagle defense with the tailback being the dive back. The fullback can align opposite the play call and be the pitchman.

Coaching Points:

- The tailback will step playside and work downhill to mesh with the quarterback.
- The quarterback will step at 45 degrees and get up in the hole.
- The center must step hard to the playside to block the noseguard.

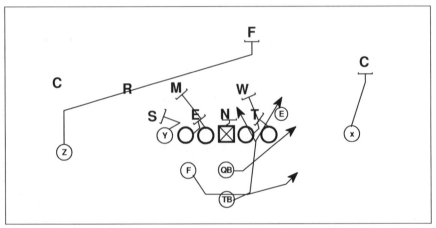

Figure 3-8

Play #23: Rip 3 Inside Veer Right

Description: The inside veer can also be run to the tight end side. When running the inside veer to the tight end side, the tight end tracks the playside inside backer. If the playside inside backer flies out quickly, the tight end will block him. Versus the 4-4 defense, the quarterback can check the veer to the side where the offense has an advantage.

Coaching Points:

- The quarterback will read the frontside defensive end.
- The tight end must get his eyes to the playside inside linebacker.
- The quarterback must get his eyes to his read.

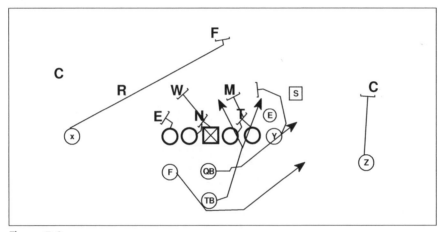

Figure 3-9

Play #24: Rip 3 Inside Veer Right vs. College 4-3

Description: The inside veer is a very good play to run to the tight end side versus a college 4-3. Because there is no C gap player, the offense will read the 9 technique. The quarterback will use the same technique to read the 9 technique as he used to read the 5 technique. The tight end will use the best release to block the Sam linebacker. If the 9 technique is wide, the tight end will use an inside release. If the 9 technique is tight, the tight end will use an outside release.

Coaching Points:

- The quarterback will read the 9 technique for his give/keep read.
- The backside back will be the pitchman.
- The offensive line must rate their hips into the hole.

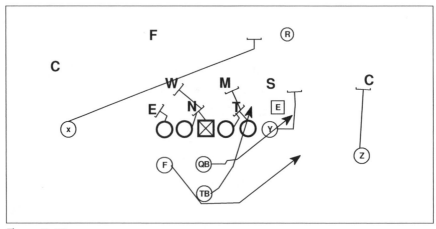

Figure 3-10

Play #25: Rip 2 X Over Veer Right vs. Under Front

Description: X over brings the X as a trips receiver to the tight end side. This forces the defense to align to the formation adjustment. You can run the veer to the X over side or away, based on the defensive adjustment. Versus an under front, the playside tackle and the tight end can work together to track the playside linebacker to the safety.

Coaching Points:

- The Y and playside tackle must get their eyes to the playside linebacker.
- The quarterback will read the 5 technique.
- The quarterback must be prepared for a quick pull pitch.

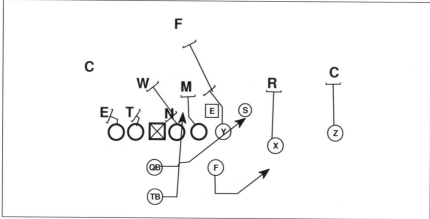

Figure 3-11

Play #26: Ron 6 Zip Veer Right Z Cowboy

Description: The veer can be run from a trips look with the Z motioning in to the formation to become the pitchman. This is a great concept to get the football into one of your best athlete's hands. This can get the football into the hands of a receiver, in a situation where they will be in the open field.

Coaching Points:

- The defense must adjust to motion.
- The quarterback must get his eyes to his read.
- Your Z has an opportunity to get the football in open space.

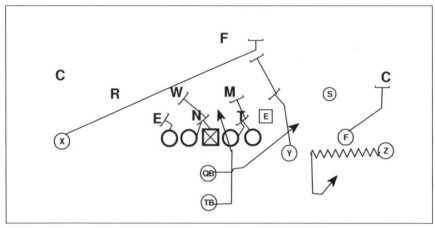

Figure 3-12

Play #27: Rip 2 Inside Veer Option Strong

Description: The inside veer strong can be run with the fullback being the dive back and the tailback being the pitchback. In Play #24, the tight end outside or arc released. Because there is no invert, the tight end will inside release to the Sam. The quarterback will read the 9 technique. If the 9 technique takes the dive back, the quarterback will pull the ball and replace the 9. If the 9 technique sits, comes upfield, or widens, the quarterback will give the football. In Play #23, the tight end outside released. Against a 3 and 9 technique, the tight end will inside release to the Sam.

Coaching Points:

- Your fullback will attack the double-team on the 3 technique.
- The tailback will be the pitchback.
- The mechanics of the play do not change.

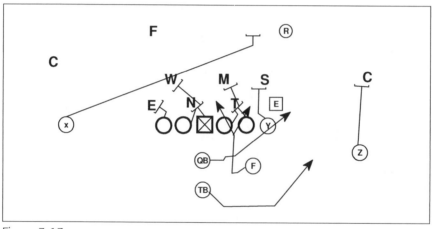

Figure 3-13

Play #28: R 7 Tom Veer Left Cowboy

Description: The tight end can be a second blocker to track the playside linebacker to safety. The playside tackle and tight end will both get their eyes to the playside linebacker. If the playside linebacker widens, the tight end will block him, and the tackle will climb to safety. The cowboy call puts the fullback as the pitchman. The Tom call puts the tight end in motion to the playside.

Coaching Points:

- Your Y becomes the second player tracking playside backer to safety.
- The fullback must ensure he gets into pitch relationship.
- The mechanics of the play do not change.

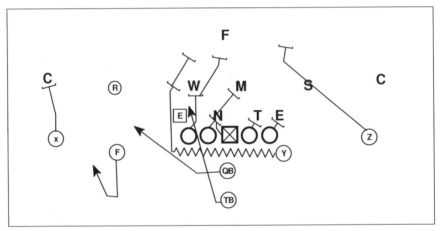

Figure 3-14

Play #29: R 5 Inside Veer Left

Description: Another way to get a second player tracking the playside inside linebacker is to flex the fullback or the Y. R puts the Y to the right side, lined up in a slot; 5 puts the fullback aligned in a slot to the left. Figure 3-15 shows the inside veer being run to the left side. The fullback is the frontside slot, and he will work with the playside tackle to track the playside inside linebacker to safety. The backside slot becomes the pitchman. Because the quarterback has depth, the backside slot does not have to go in motion. If your Y is not capable of being the pitchman, you can put in a better athlete to play that position.

Coaching Points:

- The fullback and Y will be the slot players.
- The blocking for the offensive line does not change.
- The mechanics for the quarterback and tailback do not change.

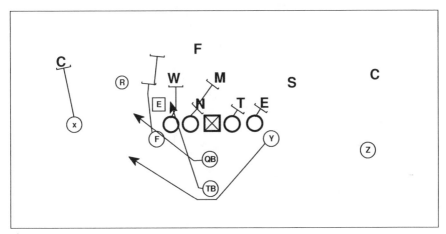

Figure 3-15

Play #30: Ron 2 Inside Veer Right

Description: The inside veer from two-back twins open is a very good concept to run. Versus balanced defenses, the offense will have an extra player on the side to which the Y lines up. Figure 3-16 shows the inside veer versus a 3-3 stack. Because the 3-3 stack is balanced, the inside veer is best run to the side of the Y.

Coaching Points:

- The quarterback will read the defensive end for his give/keep read.
- The Y and playside tackle will track the playside backer.
- The offensive line will use their veer blocking rules.

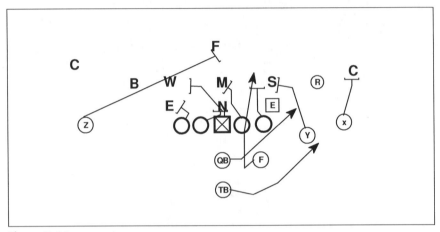

Figure 3-16

Play #31: Ron 2 Inside Veer Right vs. 3-4

Description: The 3-4 is a balanced defense, meaning the defense must adjust to the strongside of the offense. If they don't adjust, the offense should run inside veer to the strength of the formation. Figure 3-17 shows the inside veer versus the 3-4 defense. The quarterback will read the defensive end to the playside for his give/keep read, and will pitch off the outside linebacker.

Coaching Points:

- The Y must get his eyes on the playside inside backer.
- The tailback must get into pitch relationship.
- The playside tackle will use the best release.

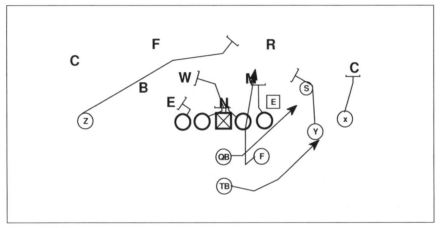

Figure 3-17

Play #32: Rip 5 Wing Inside Veer Left

Description: The wing tag moves the Z to a 1x1 wing on the tight end side. The backside wing can become the pitchman if he is to the backside of the play. Figure 3-18 shows the inside veer play to the slotside. The fullback is the second player tracking the playside linebacker. The offensive line uses inside veer blocking rules.

Coaching Points:

- The quarterback will read the C gap defender.
- The fullback must get his eyes to the playside inside backer.
- The offensive line uses inside veer blocking rules.

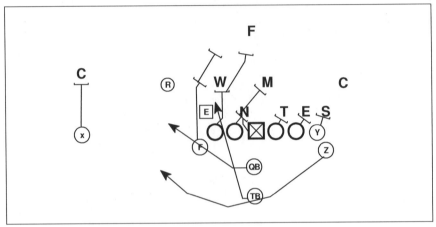

Figure 3-18

Play #33: Rip 5 Wing Inside Veer Left (Switch) vs. Overshift 4-3

Description: The switch call changes the pitch key from the force defender to the corner. The playside wide receiver will wall the invert inside, and the quarterback will attack the corner as the pitch key. The dive read remains unchanged.

Coaching Points:

- The X will crack the outside invert.
- The quarterback will pitch off the corner.
- The offensive line uses inside veer blocking rules.

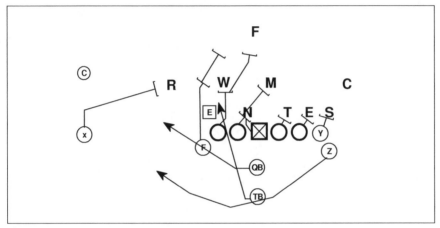

Figure 3-19

Play #34: R 5 Inside Veer Left (Switch)

Description: The inside veer switch scheme can also be run from the double slot set as well. Instead of having a wing, the offense will align the Z in his normal split receiver position. The offensive line blocks the inside veer with inside veer rules. This concept is yet another look the defense has to defend with the line blocking staying unchanged.

Coaching Points:

- The X will crack the outside invert.
- The quarterback will read the defensive end for his give/keep read.
- The offensive line uses inside veer blocking rules.

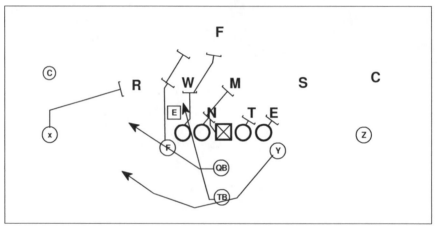

Figure 3-20

Play #35: R 2 Yap Inside Veer Left

Description: A valuable tool for the offense is to align with the strength to one side and flip the strength to the other. This is especially valuable when the defense flips players based on strength. Flexing the tight end and motioning him gives you the opportunity to get an extra blocker at the point of attack. The tight end then becomes the second player tracking the playside linebacker. Figure 3-21 illustrates the inside veer with flexed tight end motioning to the playside.

Coaching Points:

- The Y will shuffle motion to the playside.
- The quarterback will snap the ball when the Y is one yard outside the tackle.
- The reads stay the same for the offense.

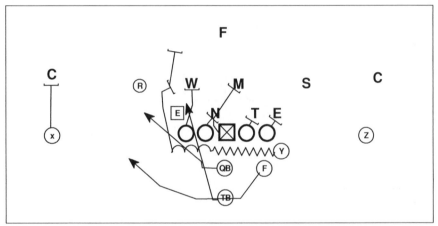

Figure 3-21

Play #36: Ron 4 Inside Veer Right Cowboy

Description: The inside veer can also be run with the inside receiver becoming the pitchman. The offense can line up in a 2x2 or 3x1 formation, run inside veer, and have the inside wide receiver drop-step and get into pitch relationship. Figure 3-22 illustrates the inside veer play being run into the trips formation, with #3 being the pitchman.

Coaching Points:

- The fullback will be the pitchman.
- The quarterback will read the defensive end for his give/keep read.
- The Y and Z will block the corner and the free safety.

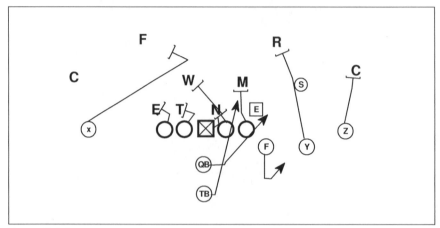

Figure 3-22

Play #37: Lou 6 Inside Veer Right Cowboy

Description: The cowboy concept can be used to a 2x2 set as well. The quarterback will read the defensive end for his give/keep read, and pitch off the force defender or alley player. The fullback will drop-step and get into pitch relationship. Figure 3-23 illustrates the cowboy concepts from a 2x2 look.

Coaching Points:

- The quarterback must reach the ball deep.
- The quarterback will read the defensive end for his give/keep read.
- The fullback must be patient to get into good pitch relationship.

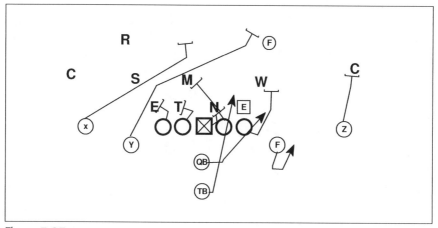

Figure 3-23

Play #38: Liz 3 Bone Inside Veer Right

Description: The pistol bone is a great look to run the midline play. To the openside, the Y becomes the second player tracking the playside linebacker. A slot or a playside back can become the second player tracking the playside linebacker. The bone forces the defense to adjust to strength, opening up opportunities to run the veer away from strength.

Coaching Points:

- The quarterback must get his eyes on his read.
- The Y must get his eyes on the playside linebacker.
- The tailback will become the pitchman.

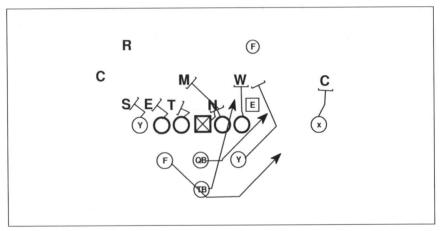

Figure 3-24

Play #39: Liz 3 Bone Inside Veer Left

Description: From the bone, the defense must be able to defend both sides of the formation. Versus a 50 defense, the veer is a good play back to the strongside. The offensive line will use their veer blocking rules. The playside back will block the cornerback. The backside back will become the pitchman.

Coaching Points:

- The quarterback must reach the ball deep and get his eyes to his read.
- The offensive line will block the inside veer the same way.
- The Y will work up to the alley support player.

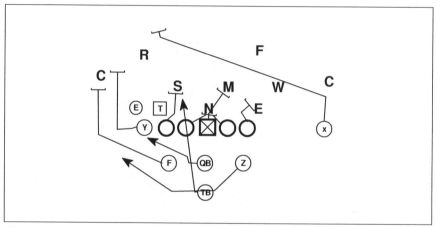

Figure 3-25

4

Load and Lead Options

The load and lead option are double option concepts that quickly attack the perimeter of the defense. The difference between the load and lead option is who you will be blocking. In the load option, the offense will load the alley player. The offensive player usually loading the alley player will normally be the fullback. The quarterback will be pitching off the end man on the line of scrimmage.

The lead option is different in that the offense will lead up onto the end man on the line of scrimmage, and the quarterback will pitch off the next defender. The load and lead options provide the offense the opportunity to get the ball out of the box quickly, forcing the defense to pursue the football.

The offensive line will block gap away on both the load and lead options. This is very similar to their veer rules. The end man on the line will not be blocked with an offensive lineman. The offensive line will use zone combination blocks to account for the down defenders and linebackers. They will rotate their hips to the hole, while driving the down defender into the linebacker.

Load Drill

The load drill teaches your running backs to read the defense and block the appropriate defender. The load is initially installed from a two-back set. The player assigned to load the alley player must understand the quarterback is pitching off the end man on the line of scrimmage. The load player will attack the pitch key and read his path. If the pitch key comes upfield, the load player will work inside him, climbing to the alley player. Figure 4-1 illustrates the load drill with the end man on the line coming upfield. If the end man on the line squeezes, the load player works outside of him up to the alley defender. Figure 4-2 illustrates the load drill with the end man on the line squeezing.

The load drill is initially done by the running backs. The coach plays the part of the read. This is a great drill to do as part of an option progression. The drill can be expanded to include the quarterback and pitchback, as well as two defenders. This allows your players to work the drill at a faster tempo. Again, initially the players must learn proper technique before the drill is run at a faster tempo.

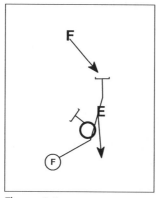
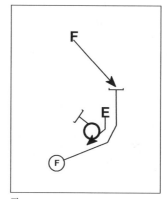

Figure 4-1   Figure 4-2

LOAD OPTION PLAYS

Play #40: Rip 2 Load Option Right vs. Overshift 4-3

Description: The load option is a tremendous play to get the ball on the perimeter quickly with blockers. Ultimately, you want to get the football to your best athletes in open space. With the load option, the offense is going to read the end man on the line of scrimmage. Versus the overshift 4-3, the offense will double-team the C gap defender to the Mike backer, while the guard will be singled up on the 3 technique. The fullback is the load player, and he will read the pitch key to determine his path to the alley player.

Coaching Points:

- The offensive line will work zone combination blocks, rotating to a leveraged backer.
- The will read the Sam for his path to the alley player.
- The quarterback will pitch off the Sam.

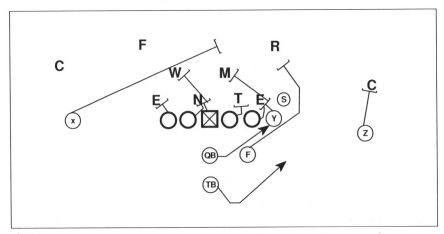

Figure 4-3

Play #41: Rip 2 Load Option Right vs. College 4-3

Description: Versus the college 4-3, the playside tight end will use best release to work up to the playside backer. The playside guard and playside tackle will combo the 3 technique to the Mike. The center and backside guard will combo the backside shade to the backside backer. The quarterback will pitch off the end man on the line of scrimmage. Figure 4-4 illustrates the load option to the tight end side versus a college 4-3 defense.

Coaching Points:

- The fullback will read the end man on the line for his path to the alley player.
- The quarterback will flash the ball then attack the inside jersey of the end man on the line.
- The frontside receiver will press the corner then engage and run.

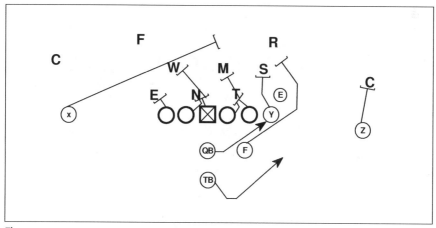

Figure 4-4

Play #42: Rip 2 Load Option Right vs. Under Front

Description: The under front gives the offensive line two zone combination blocks on the playside with leverage on the linebackers. The Sam linebacker will be the read for the quarterback, and the fullback will load the alley player.

Coaching Points:

- The Z will vertical stalk the corner.
- The tight end and tackle to the playside must get movement on the defensive end.
- The backside wide receiver sprints across the field and blocks the first threat.

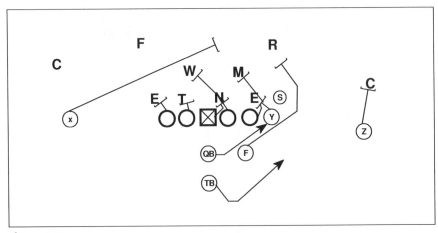

Figure 4-5

Play #43: Rip 2 Load Option
Right Switch vs. Under Front

Description: The switch call tells the playside wide receiver that he will wall the alley player. The fullback will now lead up on the corner. This gives the offense a variation to block an athletic alley player who may be difficult for your fullback to block. The read does not change for your quarterback.

Coaching Points:

- The Z will push vertical and get his eyes inside.
- The fullback will still read the end man on the line for his path.
- The quarterback will pitch off the end man on the line.

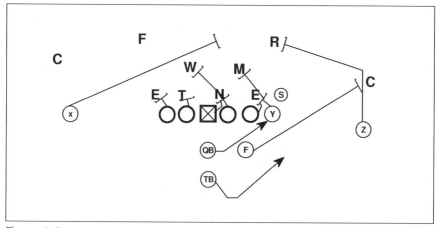

Figure 4-6

Play #44: R 3 Load Option Right Switch vs. 3-4

Description: R puts the tight end in the slot position to the right. He will follow the same blocking rules as if he was on the line of scrimmage. With the fullback in the 3 position, the load will be run with the tailback being the load blocker and the fullback being the pitchman. On the snap, the tailback attacks the end man on the line and reads him for his path. Versus the 3-4 defense, the load is a very good play. The offense has tremendous leverage running the load to the tight end side. The switch call can be made versus any defensive look, but is very effective with a cover 2 look where the corner is the force player.

Coaching Points:

- The offensive line will use zone combination blocks.
- The tailback will read the end man on the line for his path.
- The Z will release vertical before taking his path to lock the alley player.

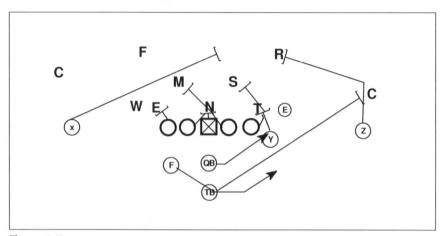

Figure 4-7

Play #45: Liz 3 Load Option Left vs. 3-3 Stack

Description: The 3-3 stack is a balanced defense, and if they do not adjust to the strength, the load option gives you tremendous leverage to the tight end side. The tight end and playside tackle will combo the defensive end to the Mike backer. The center and playside guard will double the nose. The backside guard will step hard to the playside to secure an A gap run-through and work to maintain leverage on the backside inside linebacker. The backside tackle will base block the backside defensive end. The fullback will load the playside linebacker. He is the biggest threat for the offense as he has leverage. The fullback will work off the double-team of the tight end and playside tackle, and match the path of the backer.

Coaching Points:

- The fullback will match the path of the playside backer.
- The quarterback will pitch off the invert.
- The offensive line must get four eyes to backer on their combination blocks.

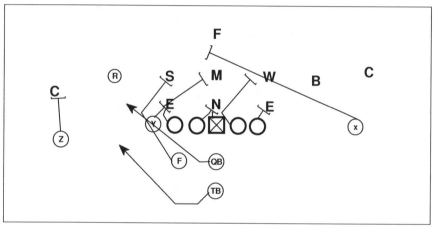

Figure 4-8

Play #46: Liz 3 Bone Hap Load
Option Left vs. Under Front

Description: The three-back pistol set is a great way to run the load option. The backside back can quickly be motioned to the playside to give you an extra blocker before the defense can adjust. To the closed side, the fullback will lead up to the corner. The motion back will become the load player.

Coaching Points:

- The backside back must motion quickly.
- The fullback must account for the corner.
- The offensive line blocking rules do not change.

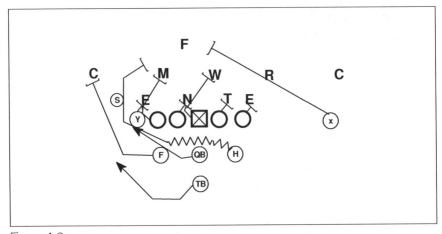

Figure 4-9

Play #47: Liz 3 Bone Load
Option Right vs. Under Front

Description: The load option can also be run away from the tight end. This essentially becomes speed option with a lead blocker. The load option weak happens much quicker. The quarterback will now pitch off the C gap player. The load player will block the first defender past the pitch read. This will sometimes be an outside linebacker aligned in an inverted position.

Coaching Points:

- To the openside, the pitch read happens much quicker.
- The frontside back must make a quick read on the end man on the line.
- The backside back will run opposite to hold the safety.

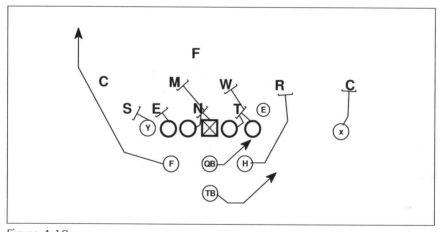

Figure 4-10

Play #48: Liz 2 Load Option Right Switch

Description: The switch call can also be used with the load option weak. If the defense has an invert outside the end man on the line, the switch call puts the playside wide receiver quickly on the invert. The fullback then works immediately to the corner.

Coaching Points:

- The quarterback must be ready for the quick pitch read.
- The load back works straight to the corner.
- The offensive line rules do not change.

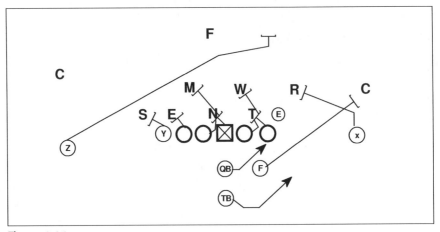

Figure 4-11

Play #49: Rip 6 Load Option Right

Description: Load can also be run from a tight end trips look. The fullback will block the first player outside the read. This will most likely be a strong safety. The blocking scheme is unchanged for the offensive line and the read does not change for the quarterback.

Coaching Points:

- The fullback will align as the inside receiver to the tight end side.
- The fullback must account for the first defender outside the read.
- The backside wide receiver will hustle to get involved in the play.

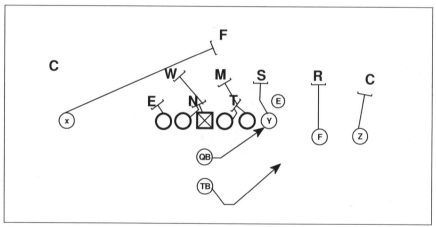

Figure 4-12

Play #50: Rip 4 Fap Load Option Left (Weak)

Description: By aligning in a wing set, you force the defense to adjust to the wing. This limits the number of ways the defense can align to your 2x2 sets. When you motion the fullback, the defense then must adjust to your motion. The ball will be snapped when the fullback clears the end man on the line. The fullback will immediately climb to block the first defender outside the read.

Coaching Points:

- The ball will be snapped when the fullback is outside the end man on the line.
- The quarterback will pitch off the end man on the line.
- The offensive line will work zone combination blocks.

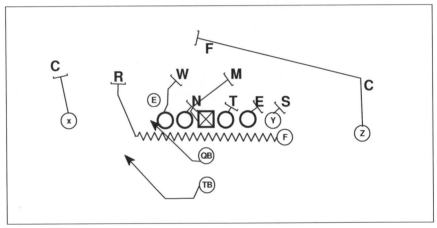

Figure 4-13

LEAD OPTION PLAYS

The lead option is a variation of the load, with the word "lead" telling the fullback he will block the end man on the line. If the end man on the line widens, the fullback will kick him out, and the quarterback will run up inside of the fullback. If the end man on the line squeezes, the fullback will log him inside, and the quarterback will pitch off the next defender. Like the load, the offense must spend time drilling the fullbacks on the lead. The fullback must be able to read the intention of the end man on the line. He must recognize whether the end man on the line is squeezing or widening.

Play #51: Rip 2 Lead Option Right vs. Overshift 4-3

Description: The offensive line will block lead the exact same way as they blocked the load option. The fullback will attack the outside jersey number of the Sam. If the Sam squeezes and works inside, the fullback will log him. If the Sam works to box the play or stay outside the fullback, the fullback will kick him out. The quarterback will read the block of the fullback to determine his path.

Coaching Points:

- The fullback will block the end man on the line of scrimmage.
- The quarterback will read the block of the fullback.
- The offensive line uses load blocking rules.

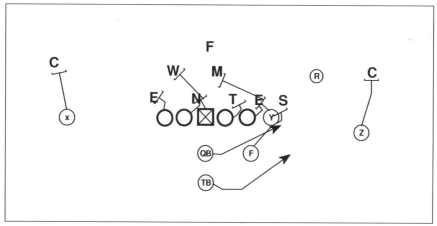

Figure 4-14

Play #52: Ron 3 Lead Option Left

Description: The lead option can also be run to the weakside of the defense. The fullback must tighten his alignment slightly. He will block the end man the same way. If the end squeezes, the fullback will lock him inside. If the end widens, the fullback will kick him out.

Coaching Points:

- The fullback must tighten his alignment.
- The quarterback will read the fullback for his path.
- The offensive line will use zone combination blocks.

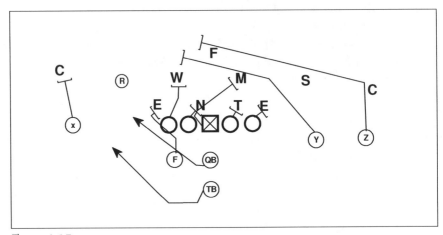

Figure 4-15

Play #53: Liz 3 Bone Lead Option Left

Description: Taz is an alert you can use that says the quarterback will mesh with both backs. The quarterback will mesh with the fullback crossing in front of him, and then he will pivot and mesh with the tailback crossing in front of him from the opposite side. The tailback must be patient to ensure the fullback has cleared the mesh point and the quarterback has time to pivot. After the quarterback gives the football to the tailback, he will sprint outside to hold the defense.

Coaching Points:

- The fullback will look to seal the end man on the line.
- The offensive line will slow rotate their combination blocks.
- The quarterback will pitch of the corner.

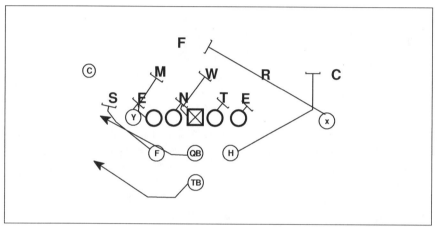

Figure 4-16

5

Zone Read Game

Zone read concepts give the offense a way to incorporate option football into the pistol offense. If the offense is not a midline, veer, load, lead, or speed option team, they can run the zone read and be able to option a defender from a traditional run play.

The zone read is run with the same zone blocking scheme as you would run with your downhill zone play. You can run the inside zone and outside zone with a read. By tagging the word read, you are choosing a defender you will not block. Instead, the quarterback will read that player.

Squeeze and Chase, Pull and Replace

When you run the zone read play, your quarterback must have a rule that he can follow when deciding whether to give or keep the football. When you run the zone read, the defender you are reading has two choices: he can attack the running back, or he can stay home and play the quarterback. If he squeezes and chases the back, the quarterback will pull the football and run through the area the defender has vacated. If the defender does anything else, the quarterback will give the football to the back and carry out a run fake after disengaging the mesh. Figure 5-1 illustrates the quarterback reading the backside end who squeezes and chases. The quarterback will pull the football and replace the read.

If the read player does anything else, the quarterback will give the football. Figure 5-2 shows the end coming upfield. Because he is not chasing, the quarterback will give the football and carry out a fake.

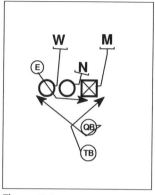

Figure 5-1

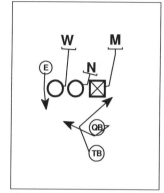

Figure 5-2

Inside Zone Read Blocking

The inside zone read play uses inside zone blocking for the offensive line. Each offensive lineman will be responsible for a gap he will be blocking. Further, a count system will help each offensive lineman to identify which player is assigned to his gap. If your offensive linemen can count to three, you can effectively run the inside zone read. Additionally, the same count system is used in the stretch read play as well.

The center is responsible for the playside A gap. The playside guard is responsible for the playside B gap. The playside tackle is responsible for the playside C gap. If a tight end is in the game, he will block the playside D gap. The backside guard has the backside A gap. The backside tackle has the backside B gap. By rule, the quarterback will read the backside C gap player.

To take this a step further, numbers are assigned each defender. The center will establish who the zero is. The zero is the first player on or over the center to the playside. Essentially, the zero is the playside A gap player. The center will draw an imaginary line down the center of the defense. He will identify who the first defender is on or over him to the playside. He then will communicate that player's identification with the rest of the offense. You can use any word you want to identify that player. The center also points as he makes his identification. Figure 5-3 illustrates the identification of the zero on the zone play to the right. If the zone play is to the left, the center will identify the first player on or over him to the left. Figure 5-4 illustrates the center identifying the zero if the zone were run left.

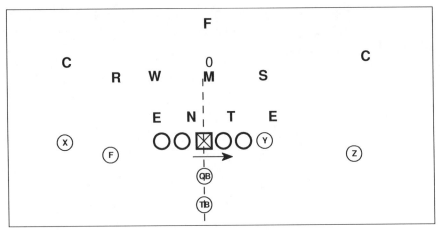

Figure 5-3

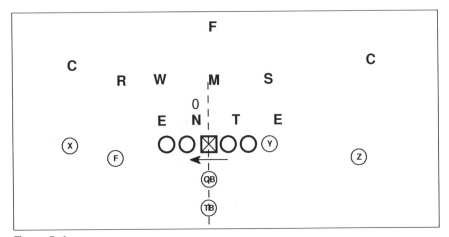

Figure 5-4

Once the center identifies who the zero is, the offense will number the defenders. The next defender to the playside will be the number 1. The next will be number 2, and the next will be number 3. The same thing happens to the backside. The first player to the backside of the play will be the number 1, the next player the number 2, and so on. Figure 5-5 illustrates the count system versus an over front.

In both the inside zone and stretch concepts, offensive linemen will be working in tandem to account for a down defender and linebacker. This process is commonly known as a covered/uncovered concept. The frontside covered lineman will be working with an uncovered lineman. This allows the offense to account for slants, stunts, dogs, and fires.

Once you have established the area you will be blocking and the threats to that area, the offensive linemen must learn footwork and landmarks. The aiming point is the playside jersey number of the defender. Both players working in tandem will have

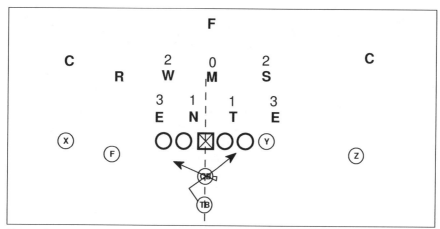

Figure 5-5

their eyes through their gap. If the right tackle and right guard are working in tandem on a 5 technique, they will both have their eyes on the 5 technique as the ball is snapped. If the 5 technique stays in the C gap, the tackle will stay on him, and the guard will climb to the linebacker. If the defender slants inside, the guard will block him, and the tackle will climb to linebacker.

Figure 5-6 illustrates the covered/uncovered concept where the down lineman slants inside. The uncovered lineman will work to the playside jersey number. The outside lineman will put pressure on the down player with his inside arm before climbing to linebacker.

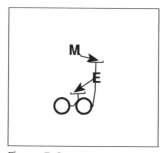

Figure 5-6

The stretch play uses the exact same count system as the inside zone for the offensive line, which allows you to use a new concept without adding new rules. The difference is the landmark of the offensive line. In the stretch play, the offensive linemen are working to get to the outside bicep of the defensive player. Ultimately, the offensive linemen would like to lock that player in the box. If they widen, the offensive linemen will keep fighting for the outside bicep and run them to the sideline. Figure 5-7 illustrates the stretch read play with a pitch phase.

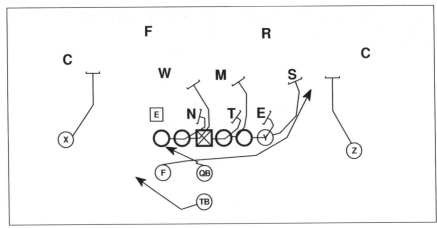

Figure 5-7

The stretch play typically will be run with an offset back, but it can also be run with the back directly behind the quarterback. The stretch play can also be run as a triple option if you have a pitchback. Often, the stretch play will not be run wide because the defense is running sideways so as to not get leveraged to the outside. Running the stretch play creates seams in the defense by forcing them to defend the width of the field.

Keep in mind that a lot more goes into blocking the inside zone and stretch. This chapter is meant to give you an overview of the concept of the zone read and stretch read. The beauty of the inside and stretch read concepts is that you can run them versus any defensive front, stunt, or blitz.

Play #54: Ron 7 Inside Read Right

Description: This is the typical 2x2 spread inside read play. The offensive line will block the inside zone. The Y and fullback will block the inverts. The receivers will block the man over them, typically a corner. It is vital to do a great job of blocking the perimeter.

Coaching Points:

- The offensive linemen will work to get to the playside jersey number of the down defender.
- The quarterback will read the backside defensive end.
- The quarterback will use the "squeeze and chase, pull and replace" rule.

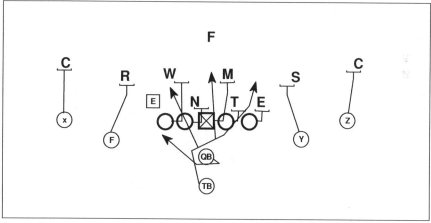

Figure 5-8

Play #55: Ron 7 Inside Read Right Cowboy

Description: The cowboy call tells the inside receiver he will drop-step and get into pitch relationship. The offensive line will follow their inside zone blocking rules. The quarterback will read the backside C gap player for his give/keep read. The cowboy tag turns the zone read into a triple option with the inside receiver. Figure 5-9 illustrates the inside zone read with a cowboy call.

Coaching Points:

- The cowboy player will drop-step, gain depth, and patiently work into pitch relationship.
- The quarterback will read the backside C gap player for his give/keep read.
- The quarterback will pitch off the invert if he gets a pull read.

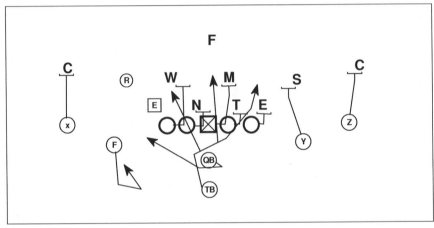

Figure 5-9

Play #56: Liz 6 Inside Read Left vs. 3-3 Stack

Description: Liz puts the tight end to the left side. Versus the 3-3 stack, the center will punch the nose to allow the backside guard to overtake the block. If the nose slants strong, the center will block him, and the backside guard will climb to the Mike linebacker. Figure 5-10 illustrates the inside zone read play to the left versus a 3-3 stack defense.

Coaching Points:

- The back will read the frontside B gap bubble for his cut.
- The quarterback will read the backside C gap player.
- The offensive line will use their covered/uncovered rules.

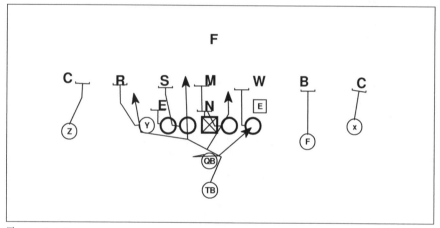

Figure 5-10

Play #57: Rip 7 Inside Read
Right Cowboy vs. Overshift 4-3

Description: The inside read play with a pitch phase is a very good concept. This play forces the defense to have a defender assigned to account for the quarterback and the pitchman. The defense also has to put enough players in the box to defender the inside zone phase.

Coaching Points:

- The quarterback reads the backside C gap defender.
- The offensive line uses inside zone blocking rules.
- The fullback drop-steps and gets into pitch relationship.

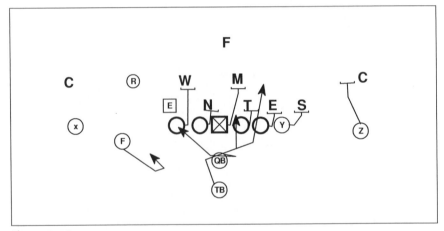

Figure 5-11

Play #58: Liz 2 Inside Read Left Option

Description: The word "option" adds a pitch phase to the inside read. The fullback will align in the backfield in Liz 2, and he will become the pitch player. The reads do not change for the quarterback, nor does the blocking for the offensive line.

Coaching Points:

- The fullback will work in 1x4 pitch relationship.
- The offensive line will use inside zone blocking rules.
- The quarterback will read the C gap defender.

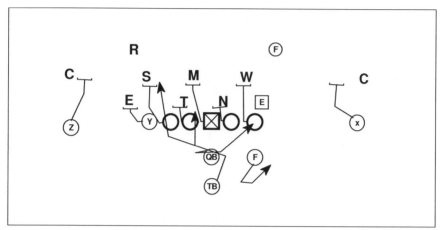

Figure 5-12

Play #59: R 3 Inside Zone Right Option

Description: The inside read play can be run with either the offset back or the tailback. With the offset back being the zone player, the tailback becomes the pitch player. The reads for the quarterback do not change, nor do the blocking rules.

Coaching Points:

- The tailback will drop-step, cross over, and get into pitch relationship.
- The quarterback will pitch off the alley player.
- The offensive line will work to get to the playside jersey number.

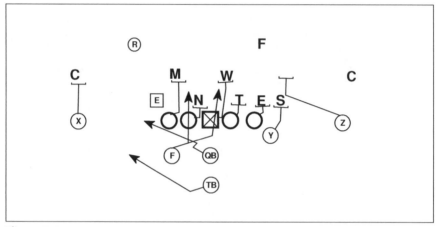

Figure 5-13

Play #60: Liz 7 Inside Read Left (Reading 3 Technique)

Description: In addition to reading the C gap player, the offense can use an alert word to read the 3 technique. The backside tackle will base block the C gap player, while the quarterback will read the defensive tackle. The read concept does not change. If the 3 technique squeezes and chases, the quarterback will pull and replace, which will be a downhill run for the quarterback.

Coaching Points:

- The backside tackle will account for the backside C gap player.
- The quarterback will read the 3 technique.
- The offensive line will follow inside zone rules.

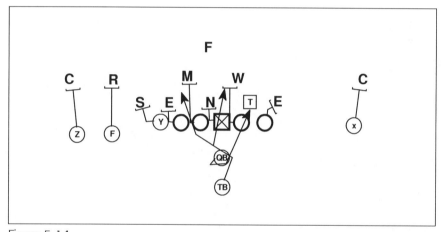

Figure 5-14

Play #61: Liz 3 Inside Read Left Boss Cobra

Description: The inside read can be run with a boss call as well. Boss alerts the fullback that he will block the strong safety or invert player. Additionally, the cobra call can be used as an alert that the quarterback will pitch off the corner. This pitch is only done to the single receiver side with no invert. This move forces the corner to make a decision. With full flow action, the defense tends to flow very fast, which opens up opportunities for a pull and pitch out the back door.

Coaching Points:

- The fullback will lead up on the alley player.
- Cobra tells the X he will be the pitchman.
- The offensive line blocking rules do not change.

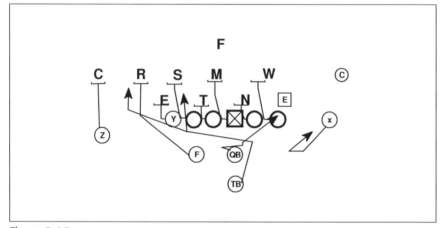

Figure 5-15

Play #62: Lou 2 Inside Read Right Bob Indian

Description: The bob call puts the lead back on the backer. The fullback will lead up on the playside backer, which turns the play into more of an isolation play. The Indian tag turns the path of the inside receiver into that of a bubble. If the quarterback gets a pull read, he will run down the line of scrimmage. If the alley player widens, the quarterback will keep the ball. If the alley player plays the quarterback, the quarterback will throw the bubble on the run.

Coaching Points:

- The Y runs the bubble path.
- The quarterback will throw the bubble off the alley player.
- The mechanics of the play do not change.

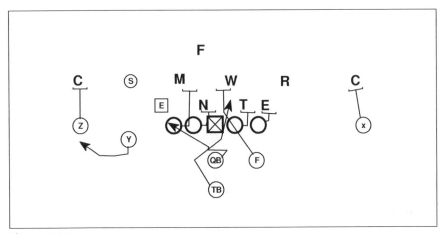

Figure 5-16

Play #63: Rip 7 Inside Read
Left Jill (Reading 3 Technique)

Description: The inside read play can also be run weak with a midline concept. The offensive line will block zone lead left, but they will not block the 3 technique. If the 3 technique squeezes and chases, the quarterback will pull and replace. The Jill call adds a fold block with the tight end and tackle. The tackle will block out, and the tackle will wrap through the B gap. If the quarterback gets a pull read, the tight end will be the lead blocker for the quarterback.

Coaching Points:

- The offensive line will leave the 3 technique unblocked.
- The quarterback must get his eyes to the read.
- The tight end must get his eyes upfield.

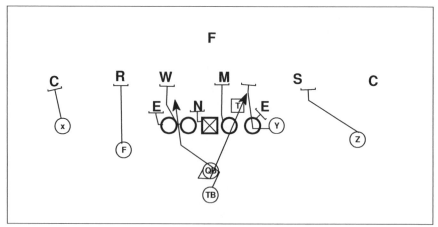

Figure 5-17

Play #64: Liz 2 Stretch Read Left Tailback Boss

Description: The stretch read play creates wide flow for the defense to defend. This play creates a great opportunity to read a fast flow defender. Reading the backside 3 technique can create a tremendous downhill run opportunity for the quarterback. With the offset back running the stretch, the play will create immediate lateral action.

Coaching Points:

- The quarterback will read the backside 3 technique.
- The tailback will block the alley player.
- The offensive line is looking to lock the box.

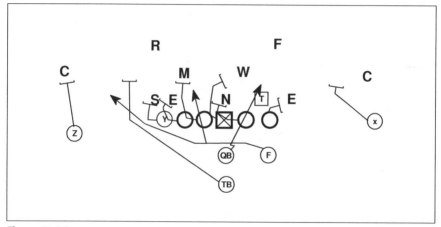

Figure 5-18

Play #65: Rip 3 Stretch Right
Tailback Crack Backer Read

Description: The stretch can also be run with the quarterback reading the backside linebacker. This play works very well reading the backside B gap backer. If the backer flows with the stretch, the quarterback will pull the football and replace the backer. The crack call puts the tailback on the corner, and the receiver cracking the alley player.

Coaching Points:

- The Z will crack the alley player.
- The tailback will block the corner.
- The quarterback must get his eyes on the linebacker he is reading.

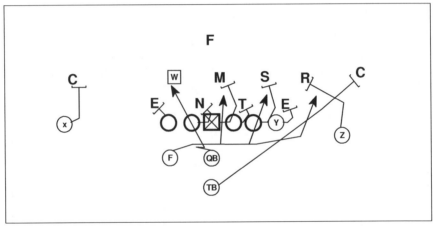

Figure 5-19

Play #66: Ricky 2 Stretch Read Left Option

Description: The stretch play can also be run away from the tight end, with the quarterback reading a tight end side player. The option tag puts the tailback as a pitch player to the backside. The offense wants to create a situation where the defense does not have enough players to play both the give/keep phase and the pitch phase.

Coaching Points:

- The fullback will read the first bubble to the edge.
- The quarterback must get his eyes to the backside read.
- The offensive line uses stretch blocking rules.

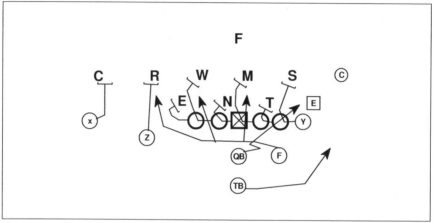

Figure 5-20

Play #67: Ricky 2 Stretch Left Nose Read Option

Description: Stretch action creates a tremendous opportunity to read the nose. With the center working fast, the nose tends to chase, which creates a huge vacant area in the center of the defense. The backside tackle and tight end must stay home and base block the backside C and D gaps. The tailback runs a pitch path to hold the backside safety. By reading different defenders, the offense can dictate who carries the ball.

Coaching Points:

- The quarterback will read the noseguard.
- The tailback must run a pitch path and get the attention of the backside safety.
- The offensive line will use stretch blocking.

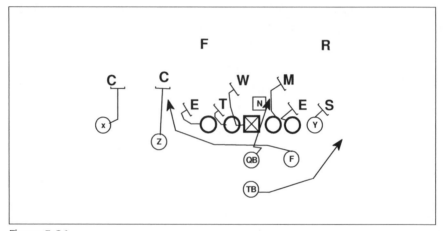

Figure 5-21

Play #68: Rex Stretch Right Read Option

Description: The bunch play forces the defense to align to the bunch or find themselves outnumbered to the weakside. With the read option game, the offense can account for multiple defenders without blocking them. The frontside fullback can either help lead the back, or he can become the pitchman. The cross key action creates conflict in the linebackers.

Coaching Points:

- The fullback will become the pitchman.
- The tailback will run the stretch path.
- The quarterback must get deeper on his first step to create space for the tailback to get width.

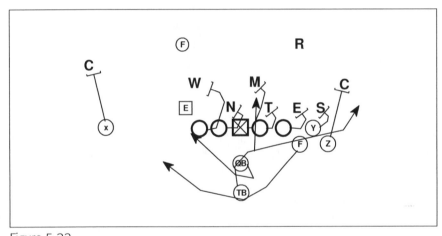

Figure 5-22

6

Trap Read Concepts

The trap play has long been a staple of powerful offenses. When defenders get upfield too far, the offense can use a trap play to take advantage of a penetrating defender. The trap play in the pistol can be run both as a downhill run play and as a read play. The trap read offers tremendous opportunities to attack the defense with leverage. The offensive line will work angle blocks with leverage. Trap blocks create seams for the running back to run, while incorporating a read forces the defense to play assignment football.

The trap read is very simple to block. The offensive will trap the first defensive lineman past the playside guard. Versus an over front defense, this lineman will often be a 3 technique if the trap is being run strong. Versus an under front, the 5 technique will often be the one being trapped to the strongside. The key component is the offensive linemen rotating their hips into the hole to create leverage on the defense. The offensive lineman, who is covered by the defender to be trapped, will release to the second level. Typically, this will be an inside release; however, it can also be an outside release. Similar to veer, you tell your offensive linemen to take the best release to account for the second-level defender.

The trap can give the offense diversity as well. The offense can adjust who is being trapped based on the defense being called. Or, the offense can adjust who is being trapped based on the defender getting the most penetration. Communication is vital to making the trap read work.

Play #69: Lou 3 Trap Right Read Option

Description: The trap read can be run as a read play or as a triple option play. The first defensive lineman past the offensive guard will be the player to be trapped. Figure 6-1 illustrates the trap read play to a 3 technique. The frontside guard will take the best release to the playside inside linebacker. The frontside tackle will base block the playside defensive end. The center will block back on the nose, and the backside guard will trap the 3 technique. This is a quick trap play, meaning the guard will not work for depth. He will stay flat and aim for the inside jersey number of the 3 technique. The backside tackle will inside release to the backside linebacker. The quarterback will mesh with the fullback. The quarterback will ride the fullback while reading the backside C gap defender. His rule remains: "Squeeze and chase, pull and replace."

Coaching Points:

- The quarterback will read the backside C gap defender.
- The offensive line will rotate their hips away from the hole.
- The trapper must aim for the inside jersey number of the defender being trapped.

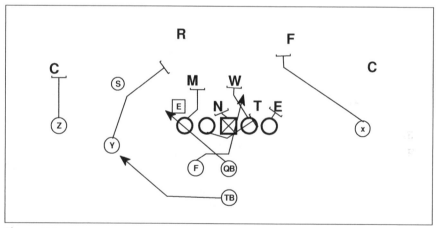

Figure 6-1

Play #70: Lou 3 Trap Right
Read (Reading 3 Technique)

Description: When the trap read is run to a nose and 5 technique, the guard will have a longer distance to travel before he gets to the defender being trapped. The difficult part of the trap versus a nose and 5 technique is the backside 3 technique. If the center blocks back on the backside 3 technique, the backside inside linebacker will not be accounted for. To account for each defender and give the offense leverage, the quarterback will change his read from the backside 5 technique to the 3 technique. This change allows the center and frontside guard to combo the nose to the backside linebacker. The backside tackle will base block the backside 5 technique. The quarterback now reads the backside 3 technique. If the 3 technique squeezes and chases the fullback, the quarterback will pull the football and get downhill. If the 3 technique does anything else, the quarterback will give the football. With the guard pulling, the 3 technique will often get in the hip pocket of the guard, which gives the quarterback a pull read. Figure 6-2 illustrates the trap read with the quarterback reading the 3 technique.

Coaching Points:

- The back must get his eyes on the trapper.
- The offensive line must communicate who is being read.
- The quarterback must get his eyes to his read on the mesh.

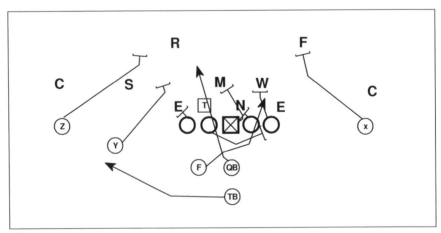

Figure 6-2

Play #71: Lou 2 Trap Left Read
Option Switch vs. Under

Description: The trap read can be run with a switch call as well. With a switch call, the corner will push crack on the alley player. The push crack works well versus cover 2, and sets up the play-action game. The offensive line blocks the trap play, while the quarterback will read the backside defensive end. If the quarterback gets a pull read, he will attack the alley and pitch off the corner.

Coaching Points:

- The playside wide receiver will release vertical before cracking on the safety.
- The quarterback will widen his path on a pull read.
- The tailback must stay in 1x4 pitch relationship.

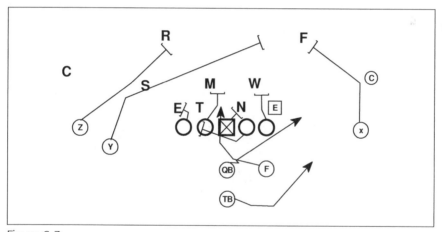

Figure 6-3

Play #72: L 3 Trap Right Read Option vs. 3-3 Stack

Description: The trap option is a very good play versus a balanced odd stack defense. If the defense stays balanced, the offense has an advantage to the Y. Because the defense is reading rather than blocking two defenders, the offense has a numeric advantage. The offensive line will block the trap play, while the quarterback will read the backside defensive end for his give/keep read. The quarterback will then pitch off the invert. The Y and the backside tackle will track the backside inside linebacker. If the backside inside linebacker widens, the Y will block him. If he works inside, the backside tackle will block him.

Coaching Points:

- The backside tackle and Y must get their eyes to the backside linebacker.
- The quarterback must get his eyes to his read.
- The trapping guard must aim for the inside jersey number of the defender he is trapping.

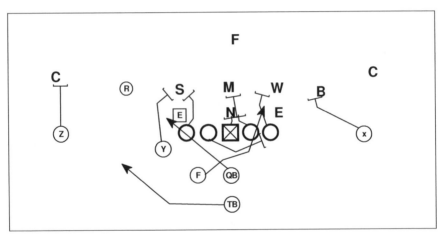

Figure 6-4

Play #73: Liz 5 Zip Trap Left Read Arc vs. 50

Description: The trap read play can be run with the tailback as well. The quarterback will use identical footwork to the inside read play. The tailback will mesh with the quarterback and get his eyes on the trapper. Versus the 5-2 or 3-4 defense, the backside guard will most likely be trapping the defensive end. The playside tackle will take the best release to block the playside linebacker. The center and frontside guard will combination block the nose to the backside backer. The arc call tells the backside tackle to outside release to the outside linebacker. The quarterback will read the backside defensive end to determine whether he gives or keeps the football.

Coaching Points:

- The Z will motion into the formation.
- The quarterback must get his eyes to his read.
- The tailback must get his eyes on the trapper.

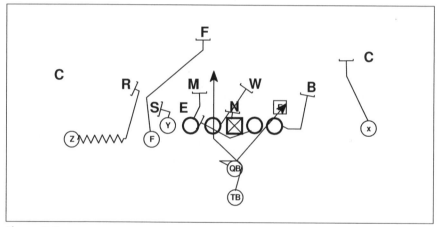

Figure 6-5

Play #74: Ricky 2 Influence
Trap Right Read Option Crack

Description: The influence trap is a very good play against linebackers who read guards. The playside inside linebacker often will flow too wide with the playside tackle zoning outside. This play also helps to keep the defensive tackle from squeezing quickly. Adding a read and a pitch phase helps the offense to force the defense to play assignment football. Figure 6-6 shows the influence trap read with a pitch phase.

Coaching Points:

- Y will release up to the safety.
- The X will crack the free safety.
- The Z will arc to block the corner.

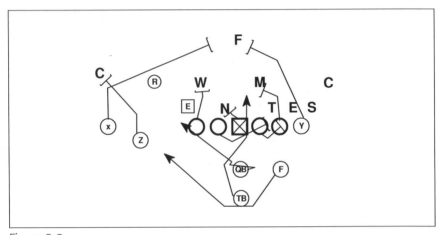

Figure 6-6

Play #75: Ron 3 Bone Trap Right Read Option Crack

Description: The trap read option can also be run from three-back sets. The frontside back will be the lead blocker, working up to the corner. The playside receiver will push crack onto the free safety. The quarterback will mesh with the tailback, while the backside back will become the pitchman.

Coaching Points:

- The quarterback can check the play either way.
- Reading the backside end gives the offense an advantage to the read side.
- The offensive line blocking rules do not change.

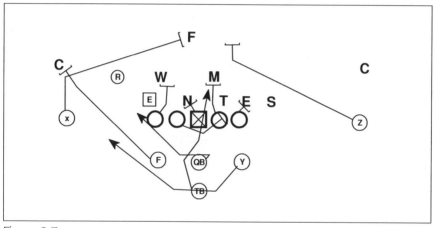

Figure 6-7

Play #76: Lou 3 Tackle Trap Right
Read Option vs. an Over Front

Description: The trap read can also be run with the tackle being the trapper. The quarterback will read the backside 5 technique for his give/keep read. The offensive line blocking rules do not change. The back will have to make a slight adjustment to allow the tackle time to get in front of him.

Coaching Points:

- The offensive line will use trap blocking rules.
- The quarterback will read the backside defensive end.
- The tailback will be the pitchman and must get into 1x4 relationship.

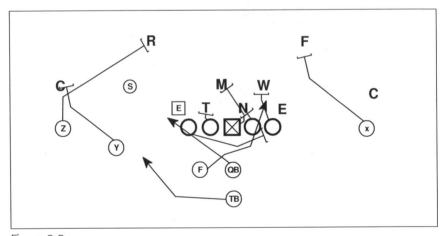

Figure 6-8

Play #77: Ron 7 Tackle Trap Right
Read Cowboy vs. an Over Front

Description: The tackle trap can also be run with the tailback. From a 2x2 set, a pitch phase can be added with the cowboy call. Cowboy alerts the backside #2 receiver that he will be the pitchman. He will drop-step, backpedal, and get into pitch relationship. You can also have him run a bubble path and gain more width.

Coaching Points:

- Cowboy tells the backside inside wide receiver that he will be the pitchman.
- The quarterback will read the backside 5 technique.
- The backside invert is the pitch read.

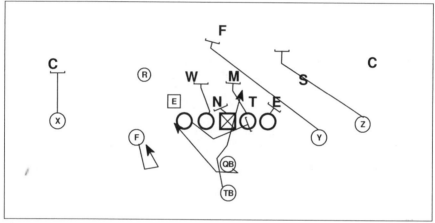

Figure 6-9

Play #78: Rip 5 Wing Tackle Trap Right Read Option

Description: The tackle trap play can be run from the bone as well. The play can be run strong or weak, with the quarterback reading a backside defender. Figure 6-10 illustrates the tackle trap read from the wishbone. The frontside fullback will get his eyes to the backside Will. If the Will flows fast with the trap, the fullback will climb to safety. If the Will widens on a stunt, the fullback will lock him in the box.

Coaching Points:

- The fullback must get his eyes on the playside linebacker.
- The backside Z will be the pitchman.
- The quarterback must reach the ball deep on the mesh.

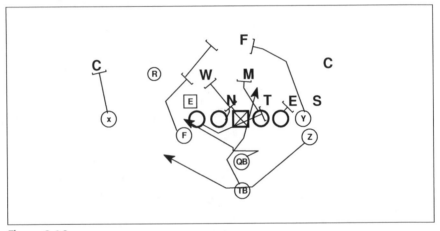

Figure 6-10

Play #79: Rip 5 Wing Tackle Wham Right Read Option

Description: A great play versus an active nose is the wham variation. The wham puts the tackle trapping the frontside noseguard. If the noseguard is getting upfield, the wham variation is a great complement. The quarterback will still read the backside defensive end. The frontside fullback will track the playside linebacker to safety, and the Z will be the pitchman.

Coaching Points:

- The quarterback must push away to get off the midpoint.
- The tailback will work downhill.
- The frontside guard will open step and gain width to influence the shade.

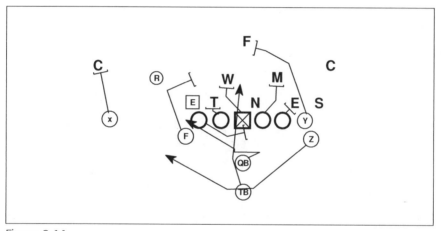

Figure 6-11

Play #80: Rip 2 Trap Same Side Trap Read Option Right

Description: Another form of the trap read is the same side concept. The quarterback will mesh with the frontside back on a downhill path. The backside guard will pull and find the defensive end. If the defensive end widens, the tackle will kick the end, and the quarterback will give the football. If the end squeezes, the guard will log the end, and the quarterback will pull the ball and pitch off the next man. This concept forces the defensive end to adapt to another look.

Coaching Points:

- The backside guard must get his eyes to the end man on the line of scrimmage.
- The quarterback and tailback will carry out the mesh on the frontside of the play.
- The quarterback will read the end man on the line of scrimmage.

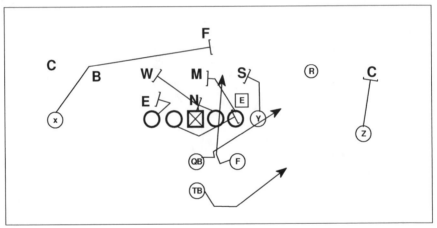

Figure 6-12

7

Counter Read Concepts

As the defense begins to aggressively flow to the football, the counter read becomes a tremendous play. The counter read can be run from a variety of formations, with the same diversity of reads as the inside read and trap read. The counter read ties in nicely with the traditional counter play as well run from the pistol.

The blocking rules for the counter read are very simple. The frontside rules for the offensive line are to zone away from the call. If you are running counter to the right, the right side offensive line will zone to the left. The backside guard and tackle will pull. The guard will kick out the end man on the line. The tackle will lead up to the playside linebacker. The offense can also have a Y or fullback replace either of the pullers, allowing that player to stay home and block on the backside.

The reads concepts are the same in the counter read as they are in the trap read and zone read. The base read is the backside C gap defender. If he squeezes and chases, the quarterback will pull and replace. If he does anything else, the quarterback will give the football to the running back. With the counter read, the quarterback will read the end man on the line of scrimmage or the backside linebacker.

Play #81: Liz 7 Counter Left Read

Description: The counter read play can be run from any formation. The frontside of the line will zone away from the play. Versus a 3 and 9 technique to the playside, the tight end will immediately release inside to wall the Mike backer. The frontside guard and tackle will drive the 3 technique to the backside backer. The backside guard will pull flat to kick out the 9 technique. The backside tackle will pull and lead through the window up to the playside linebacker. The quarterback will push off the midpoint and get his eyes to his read. He will read the 5 technique. Figure 7-1 illustrates the counter read play versus a 4-3 defense.

Coaching Points:

- The offensive linemen will zone to the backside.
- The backside guard must stay flat as he pulls.
- The quarterback will read the backside defensive end.

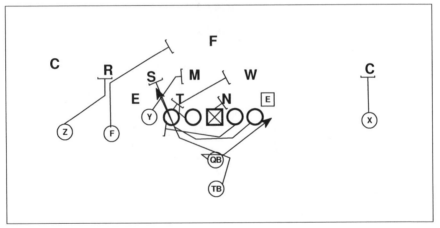

Figure 7-1

Play #82: Liz 7 Zip Counter Left Tag Read

Description: An alternative method of running the counter read is the tag scheme. Tag replaces the backside guard with the playside guard. The playside guard will pull and kick out. The backside tackle will pull and lead through. The backside guard will climb to the backside backer. This adjustment is made if the backside linebacker is staying home to play the quarterback. The offense now has a player to account for him.

Coaching Points:

- The backside tackle will reduce his split.
- The frontside guard must stay flat.
- The quarterback will read the defensive end.

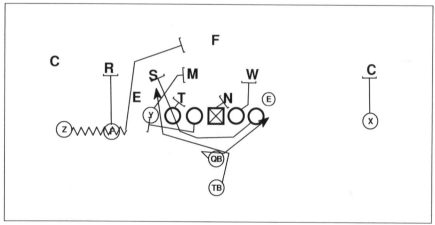

Figure 7-2

Play #83: Ricky 2 Counter Right
Read Option Switch vs. Overshift 4-3

Description: From a two-back set, the counter read can be run as an option. It can be run both strong and weak. Versus an under front, the offensive line will kick out the 5 technique because of the natural bubble created by the defense. The switch call puts the backside wide receiver push cracking the safety, and the inside wide receiver working to the corner.

Coaching Points:

- The quarterback will read the backside defensive end.
- The tailback must find the first puller and run off his hip.
- The backside back will be the pitchman.

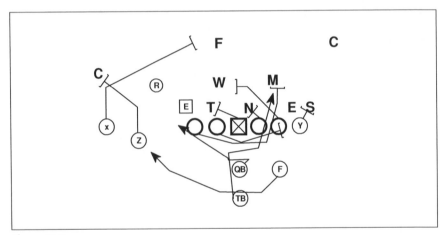

Figure 7-3

Play #84: Rip 3 Zap Fullback Counter Right Read Option vs. College 4-3

Description: The counter play can also be run with the fullback as the counter back, and the tailback as the pitchback. This approach helps to alleviate tendencies, and forces the defense to be prepared to defend both backs. The tailback will be the pitchback. The outside wide receiver will block the corner, and the inside wide receiver will block the safety. The offense can align in a twins set, or motion the Z into twins. Figure 7-4 illustrates the counter read with the fullback.

Coaching Points:

- The Z will motion full speed across the formation.
- The quarterback should snap the ball when the Z is four yards outside the tackle.
- The quarterback will read the backside C gap defender.

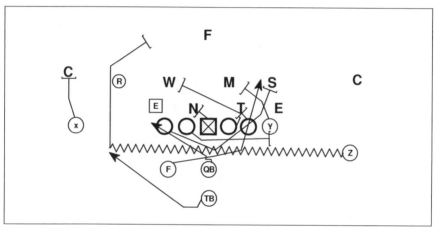

Figure 7-4

Play #85: Rip 3 Counter Left (Weak) Read Option

Description: The counter play can also be run to the weakside, with the quarterback reading the strongside. The offense can leave both the 5 and 9 technique unblocked, or they can block the 5 and leave the 9 for the quarterback to read. Figure 7-5 illustrates the counter read play with the strongside guard and tackle pulling. The quarterback is reading the strongside 5 technique, and pitching off the strongside 9 technique.

Coaching Points:

- The play will happen quicker to the weakside.
- The pulling guard must aim for the inside jersey number of the end man on the line.
- The quarterback must be drilled to respond to a quick pull/pitch.

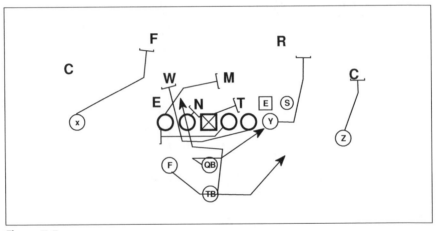

Figure 7-5

Play #86: Rip Zero Counter Hoss Right Read (Reading Tackle)

Description: Another variation to the counter read is the hoss tag. Hoss has the fullback being the second puller, leading up on the playside linebacker. This approach allows the quarterback to read the backside 3 technique. If the 3 technique is getting in the hip pocket of the pulling guard, this play becomes devastating. Figure 7-6 illustrates the counter hoss read.

Coaching Points:

- The fullback will pull and lead through on the first opposite-colored jersey.
- The quarterback will read the backside 3 technique.
- The play has no pitch key.

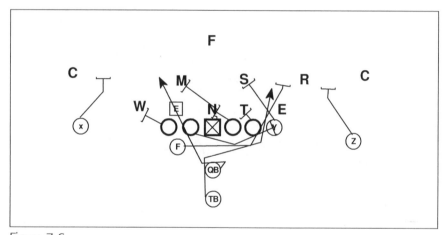

Figure 7-6

Play #87: Ron 4 Counter Right Read Option

Description: The counter read can also be run with a backside receiver as the pitchman. Figure 7-7 illustrates the counter read with the backside fullback working to be the pitchman. The mechanics of the play are unchanged, forcing the defense to defend the weakside alley.

Coaching Points:

- The fullback must be fast to get into pitch relationship.
- The quarterback will mesh with the tailback.
- The offensive line rules are unchanged.

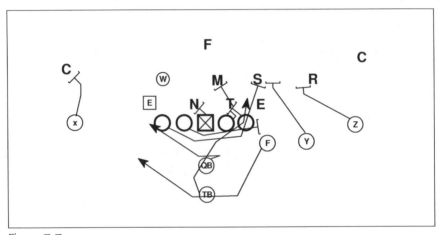

Figure 7-7

Play #88: R Zero Counter Hogg Left Mike Read

Description: With the fullback and Y both aligned to one side, the defense often will adjust. This adjustment opens up the opportunity to run the counter play with the fullback and Y being the pullers. The tackle has a key block, as he must get his eyes to the Mike. If the Mike flows, he will block him. If the Mike sits, the tackle will climb to the free safety. With the fullback and Y pulling, the backside guard and tackle will base block on the backside. The quarterback will read the Mike linebacker. If the Mike flows, the quarterback will pull the football and run downhill. If the Mike sits, the quarterback will give the football.

Coaching Points:

- The playside tackle must get his eyes to the Mike.
- The quarterback must get a good ride to give the Y time to clear the back.
- The quarterback must run downhill on a pull read.

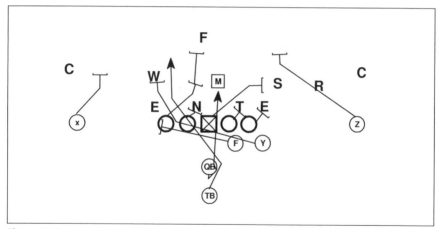

Figure 7-8

Play #89: Ron 7 Counter Right Read Option Cowboy

Description: The cowboy technique can be used with the counter read as well. The backside inside receiver will drop-step and get into pitch relationship. He will be the pitchman for the quarterback.

Coaching Points:

- The pitchman must be patient getting into pitch relationship.
- The quarterback will read the backside defensive end.
- The frontside guard and tackle must get movement on the 3 technique.

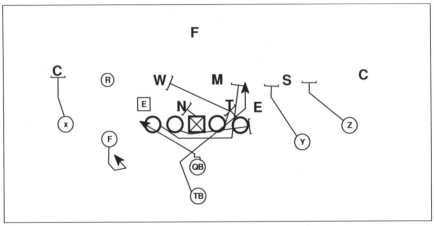

Figure 7-9

Play #90: Lou 2 Bone Counter
Hoss Right Read Option

Description: The counter read is a good play to run from the wishbone as well. The offset back away from the play can be the pull lead through player. The offset back to the callside will come around and become the pitchman. The quarterback will mesh with the tailback. The hoss tag allows the backside tackle to climb to the backside linebacker.

Coaching Points:

- The quarterback and tailback will mesh.
- The quarterback will read the backside defensive end.
- The backside fullback must get into 1x4 relationship.

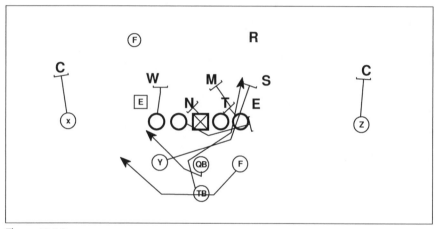

Figure 7-10

Play #91: Lou 2 Bone Counter Right Read Option

Description: When the counter read is run from the bone without a hoss tag, the backside back will lead up on the backside inside linebacker.

Coaching Points:

- The quarterback will use the "squeeze and chase, pull and replace" rule.
- The quarterback will pitch off the alley running safety.
- The backside fullback must get into 1x4 relationship.

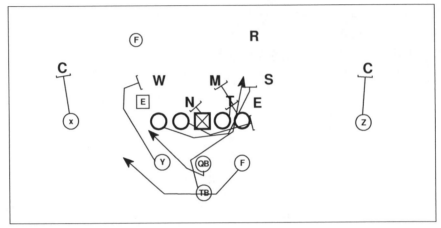

Figure 7-11

8

Shovel Option Concept

The shovel option attacks the perimeter of the defense while giving them a different look to contend with. The shovel option has the quarterback showing a wide run action, wider than speed option. The quarterback will work for more width rather than attacking the line of scrimmage. If the player the quarterback is reading widens or comes upfield, the quarterback will shovel the ball to a player working underneath. If the defender stays inside, the quarterback will keep the football and attack the alley player.

The shovel concept can be versatile for the offense. The read player can be adjusted based on game play, as can the blocking scheme. The shovel can be run from a veer blocking scheme, as well as a power blocking scheme. Regardless of which blocking scheme is employed, the mechanics of the play are virtually unchanged.

Play #92: R 2 Yap Shovel
Option Left (Veer Blocking)

Description: The quarterback will take a flat path gaining width, forcing the C gap defender to make a choice. If he widens, the quarterback will shovel the ball to the fullback coming underneath. If he squeezes, the quarterback will keep the ball and pitch off the alley player. The Y is in motion across the formation to give the offense another blocker at the point of attack. The fullback must take a path hugging the double-team. In this case, he must hug the double-team of the playside guard and center on the shade.

Coaching Points:

- The center and playside guard must have four eyes on the Mike.
- The quarterback must stay flat.
- The fullback must hug the double-team.

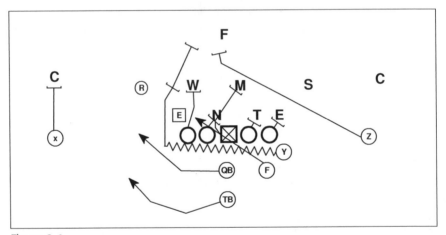

Figure 8-1

Play #93: Rex Shovel Left
(Veer Blocking) vs. Overshift 4-3

Description: Rex tells the fullback, Y, and Z that they will be bunched to the right side. The Y will align two yards outside the tackle. The fullback will align one yard off the line and one yard outside the tackle. The Z will align one yard behind the tight end and one yard outside him. The quarterback will work flat to the playside. The fullback will open and sprint, hugging the double-team on the nose. The quarterback will read the defensive end for his shovel read. He will then pitch off the next defender. This concept is great against teams that rotate their coverage to the bunch.

Coaching Points:

- The fullback must adjust his alignment based on his ability.
- The playside tackle must account for the playside inside linebacker.
- The quarterback must commit on his third step.

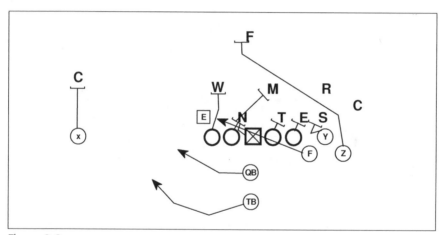

Figure 8-2

Play #94: Ron 4 Empty Slot
Shovel Right Cowboy (Mike Read)

Description: The shovel can also be run from an empty set, to either the trips or the twins side. The shovel can also be run with the quarterback reading the Mike linebacker. If the Mike widens, the quarterback will shovel the ball. If the Mike stays inside, the quarterback will work to the next defender. The fullback will use a cowboy technique, where he becomes the pitchman. The tailback will align in a slot to the left. He will run flat, hugging the double-team on the 1 technique. The playside tackle has a key block as he must reach the 5 technique.

Coaching Points:

- The playside tackle must reach and lock the playside defensive end.
- The quarterback must get his eyes to the playside inside linebacker.
- The quarterback can check the play to the best side numerically.

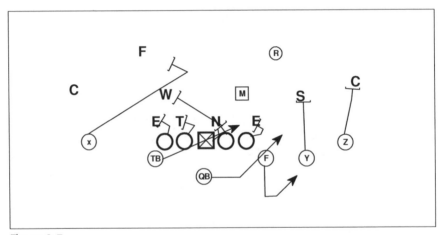

Figure 8-3

Play #95: Ron 3 Power Shovel Option Right (Power Blocking)

Description: The shovel play can also be run with power blocking. Instead of having a player kick out the end man on the line, the quarterback will option the end man on the line. This play is outstanding versus a 3-3 stack defense. The playside tackle will release to the Mike linebacker. The playside guard and center will double-team the noseguard to the backside backer. The backside guard will pull and lead through. If the playside inside backer steps up, he will block him. If he flows away, the backside guard will climb to the safety. Figure 8-4 illustrates the shovel versus the 3-3 stack.

Coaching Points:

- The Y will tighten his alignment slightly.
- The Y will work vertical three steps before taking his eyes inside.
- The quarterback will read the end man on the line for his shovel read.

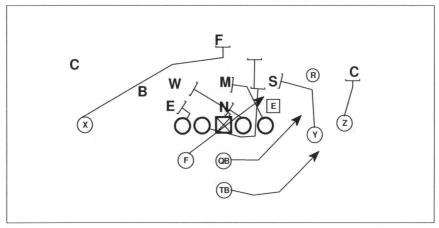

Figure 8-4

Play #96: Rip 3 Power Shovel Right vs. 4-3

Description: The shovel is a very good play with power blocking to the college 4-3. The tight end will release on an angle to cut off the Mike linebacker. The playside tackle and playside guard will combo the 3 technique to the backside backer. The backside guard will pull and get his eyes on the playside inside backer. He must stay vertical when he blocks the linebacker to allow the back to make a decision on where he will cut. The quarterback will read the end man on the line to determine whether he will pitch the football to the fullback, or keep the ball and work to the alley player.

Coaching Points:

- The fullback must make sure the backside guard gets in front of him.
- The quarterback will read the defensive end to determine whether he will pitch or keep the ball.
- The backside guard must stay square when he approaches the playside linebacker.

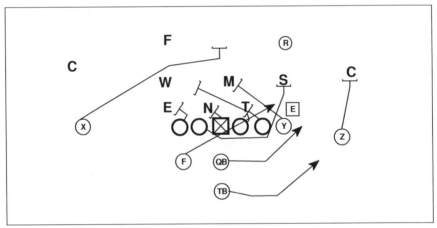

Figure 8-5

9

Frontside Read Concepts

The final piece of the option game from the pistol is the frontside read game. The frontside read gives the defense yet another concept they must prepare for. The frontside read game is versatile and can be run from a variety of sets with multiple blocking schemes. The beauty of this concept is in the simplicity. You can take a frontside play you are already running and add the read.

The frontside read play is a combination of three plays in one. You can run jet sweep, power, and iso all in one play. If the defense reacts to the jet sweep, the play can become quarterback isolation play. Or, you can use power blocking, resulting in a wide sweep or quarterback power. The great thing is: the defense never knows who you are reading. You can force the defense to spend a great deal of time preparing for this concept.

Play #97: Rip 3 Jet Sweep Read Iso Left

Description: The first concept is built off the jet sweep. The quarterback will take the snap and reach the ball into the belly of the jet player in the frontside A gap. The quarterback will then snap his eyes to the 5 technique. If the 5 technique widens, the quarterback will pull the football and follow the fullback. The fullback is leading up on the frontside inside linebacker, which essentially creates an isolation play for the quarterback if he pulls the football. If the end sits or squeezes, the quarterback will give the football to the Z. The tailback is leading up on the alley player. The playside tackle is going to outside release and get his eyes to the playside inside linebacker. If the playside backer widens, he will block him. If he stays inside, the tackle will continue working downfield to block the next support player.

Coaching Points:

- The playside tackle must get a wide release.
- The quarterback must ride, slide, and decide.
- The fullback must get downhill quickly.

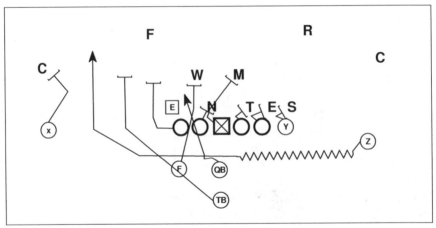

Figure 9-1

Play #98: Rip 3 Jet Sweep Power Read Left Crack

Description: This same frontside read concept can be used with power blocking as well. The quarterback will read the Z on the jet sweep while reading the end man on the line. The offensive line will block the play as if it is power to the openside. The playside tackle and playside guard will combo the 3 technique to the backside backer, which gives them tremendous leverage. The center will block back on the shade, while the backside guard will pull and lead up on the playside linebacker. If the end widens, the play becomes quarterback power. If the end sits or squeezes, the offense is running jet sweep with the secondary accounted for. The crack tag puts the playside receiver push cracking the safety. The tailback will work immediately to the corner. Figure 9-2 illustrates this concept.

Coaching Points:

- The jet player must read the alley.
- The playside receiver must push vertical before working to the safety.
- The backside guard must play with his eyes.

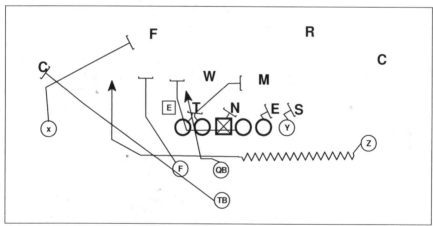

Figure 9-2

Play #99: Rip 7 Jet Zone Nose Read Left Switch

Description: Another great variation is using zone blocking with jet action. This approach allows the quarterback to read an inside defender. The quarterback will read the first down defender to the playside. If the nose widens, the quarterback will pull the ball and get downhill. If the nose stays at home, the quarterback will give the football.

Coaching Points:

- The Z must run full speed in motion.
- The quarterback will ride, slide, and decide.
- The tailback must get the alley player blocked.

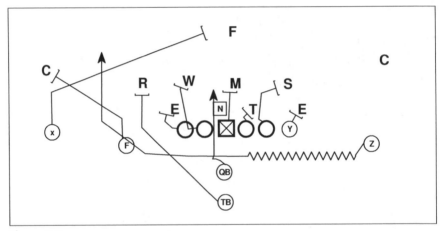

Figure 9-3

Play #100: Ron 4 Fullback Jet Sweep Left Backer Read Switch

Description: The jet sweep action can be run with your fullback as well. With the offense in a trips set, and the fullback in a slot, the offense can run jet quickly, which gives the defense little time to adjust. The quarterback can read the end man on the line, or he can read a linebacker. If the linebacker widens, the quarterback will pull the football and get downhill. If the linebacker stays inside, the quarterback will give the ball on the jet. The playside tackle will reach the defensive end and get him hooked. Figure 9-4 illustrates the jet sweep concept reading the playside linebacker.

Coaching Points:

- The fullback will be the jet player.
- The quarterback will take his eyes to the backer he is reading.
- The playside wide receiver will push crack the alley player.

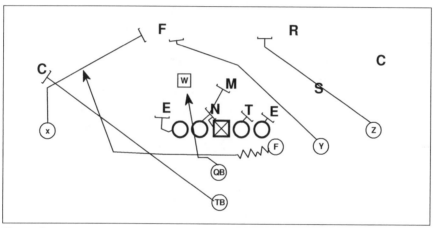

Figure 9-4

Play #101: Ricky Tight Jet Left
Defensive Tackle Read Special

Description: The jet player can also be lined up in the backfield. When the fullback is offset to the tight end side, the defense must put enough players on that side of the ball to account for the option game strong. Putting twin receivers away from the tight end forces the defense to balance up, which gives the offense an opportunity to run the football either way. By reading a frontside defender, the offense has an extra player at the point of attack. The offense can read the frontside 3 technique to determine whether the ball is given to the back running a wide path. This read gives the offensive line good leverage for blocking the remaining box players. The term "special" is a tag that says the tailback will come off his blocking path, and will become a pitchman. The offensive player running the jet will have the option to pitch the football. This option causes confusion in the defense, and takes advantage of teams that like to blitz their corner on jet sweep action.

Coaching Points:

- The quarterback will get his eyes on the frontside defensive tackle for his give/keep read.
- The tailback must be patient getting into pitch relationship.
- The offense must communicate who they are reading.

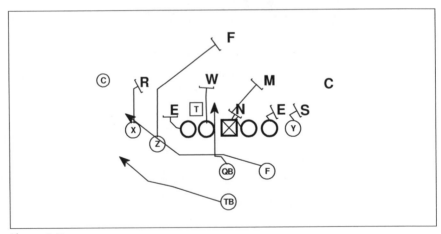

Figure 9-5

About the Author

James Vint has been both an offensive and defensive coordinator at the high school and collegiate levels, and currently is defensive line coach and special teams coordinator at Coronado High School, a 5A school in Lubbock, Texas. Previously, Vint was an assistant coach at Truman State University and the offensive coordinator at Iowa Wesleyan College, where he and his offensive staff were on the forefront of developing the pistol offense.

Prior to his stint at Iowa Wesleyan, Vint served on the coaching staff at Christopher Columbus High School in the Bronx, New York, where he helped turn around a gridiron program that had a 20-game losing streak. In his second season at Columbus, the Blue Steel qualified for the playoffs for the first time in school history, a feat that they achieved four times over a six-year period. During his five seasons on the Columbus staff (2000-2004), the Blue Steel offense averaged 256 yards per game on the ground.

Vint is a widely sought-after speaker at clinics throughout the country, and has been featured on a number of well-received instructional DVDs on the pistol offense.